Trevor Huddleston was born in 1913, and educated at Lancing and Christ Church, Oxford. The social problems of England in the early thirties quickly awoke an interest in missionary work, and he went to Ceylon and India and then to Wells Theological College.

He was ordained in 1937, and joined the Community of the Resurrection in 1939. Four years later he was sent to South Africa to the Community's Mission in Sophiatown where his enormous success among the Africans soon alarmed the authorities.

In 1956 he was recalled to England, and before he left he determined to try and assess his feelings for Africa. The outcome was *Naught for Your Comfort*, a book which awoke a world-wide interest in the plight of non-whites in Africa.

Back in England, Father Huddleston's name quickly became a household word, and the publicity he received helped to focus attention on events in South Africa.

In 1960 he was elected Bishop of Masasi in Tanganyika. Once again he has dedicated himself with energy and enthusiasm to the future of Africa and to the future of Christianity. He hopes not only to help build up the social services in Africa but also to awaken an active and world-wide response to the doctrine of the universal brotherhood of man in Christ; to remind us that 'as Christians, we are members of a Body that can know no racial barriers.'

by the same author
NAUGHT FOR YOUR COMFORT

TREVOR HUDDLESTON, C.R.

BISHOP OF MASASI

The True and Living God

Collins
FONTANA BOOKS

First published in Fontana Books, 1964

The author and publishers wish to thank the following for permission to quote from the publications indicated:

Cambridge University Press: *Soundings*, edited by A. R. Vidler; Chatto & Windus Ltd: *Island*, by Aldous Huxley; The Executors of the J. M. Murry Estate and Jonathan Cape Ltd: *Love, Freedom and Society*, by John Middleton Murry; A. R. Mowbray & Co. Ltd: *Visible and Invisible*, by Giovanni Miegge; Victor Gollancz Ltd: *The God of a Hundred Names*, edited by Victor Gollancz, and *The Church of England*, by Paul Ferris; The Sunday Times: 'Morals in Confusion'; George Weidenfeld & Nicolson Ltd. and the Atheneum Press: *The Image*, by Daniel J. Boorstin; Cambridge and Oxford University Presses: *The New English Bible*; SCM Press: *Letters and Papers from Prison*, by Dietrich Bonhoeffer; Miss Constance Babington-Smith: *The Towers of Trebizond*, by Rose Macaulay.

© *Trevor Huddleston, 1964*
Printed in Great Britain
Collins Clear-Type Press
London and Glasgow

For
St Joseph's College, Chidya, Tanganyika,
where these addresses were prepared
and for
The Very Reverend Cuthbert Simpson, D.D.
Dean of Christ Church, Oxford,
who gave me generous and kindly
hospitality while they were being delivered

CONTENTS

PREFACE

This book is made up of the eight addresses which formed
the basis of a mission to Oxford University in the Hilary
Term 1963. They appear almost exactly as they were delivered, and I have thought it best to leave them in their
original form. In other words, they were written to be
spoken to an audience of undergraduates: they were not written to be read by a much wider and more diversified public.
This must be my excuse to those who may find the style too
conversational or the vastness of the subject too briefly
handled.

I can only hope that in spite of these drawbacks, something
of what I have tried to say about God, Man and the World
may prove to be of value, if only for a little while. And I
would beg the reader's prayers for the diocese of Masasi,
Tanganyika.

✠ TREVOR MASASI
MAY 1963

I. THE WORLD

This week's activity has been described as a 'Mission to the University,' and perhaps in some ways that is a pity. The word 'mission' in England, like the word 'missionary' in Africa, is beginning to have associations with the past which make it unacceptable. Why should the Christian, any more than the Humanist or the Marxist or the Muslim, claim the right to be 'sent' by some authority or other to people who may not have any desire to receive him? And why should it any longer be assumed that what he is 'sent' to say has a relevance to their present situation which is greater than that of other ideologies? Or, perhaps at a deeper level, is there anything left to say, after nearly two thousand years, to a world which is only too well aware of the problems of modern existence and of the apparent failure of the Christian Church to reach the heart of man with a fully satisfactory answer?

May I begin on a personal note, and disclaim from the very start any special qualifications for tackling this extraordinarily difficult and dangerous job? I am not a trained philosopher, nor, except in the most elementary sense, can I claim to be anything of a theologian. When I was asked to give these addresses I made these points clear to those who had invited me, and when I pressed them further as to why they had invited me I was told that I could count on the help of philosophers and theologians in the University. What was primarily required of me was that I should speak from my own experience of living the Christian life in the context of the present age.

And when I asked the leader of the last Mission to Oxford —the present Archbishop of Canterbury—what he thought I should talk *about*, he said: 'You can talk about God. . . . Yes . . . you can talk about God!'

And that is what I'm going to try to do. But it is the hardest thing in the world to do effectively, and I am absolutely certain that I shall fail. I am certain of this, because I know far better than any of you my own limitations: and I know, perhaps better than some of you, the utter inexpressibility, the tongue-tying silence of the mystery which is God's being and presence and power. Nevertheless, I must try. I must try, simply because I believe that even the poorest expression of the truth that is in Christ is infinitely richer than the *unreality* which threatens to engulf us all. I believe, with Charles Péguy, that 'the worst of partialities is to withhold oneself, the worst ignorance is not to act, the worst lie is to steal away.' In choosing as the title of these addresses 'The True and Living God' I have a double purpose. On the one hand I want to emphasize my belief in the emptiness, the unreality, the 'absurdity' (to use a phrase of Jean-Paul Sartre) of life as lived by modern Western man. On the other, I want to proclaim as the foundation of the whole Christian apologia that it answers this absurdity with Truth and this emptiness with Life. And I want to attempt to show you this not by an appeal to philosophy in the abstract or to theology in the abstract but by an appeal to experience. I recognize the dangers! This kind of approach must mean that I speak about myself; and therefore it can look horribly like plain arrogance. Moreover, it must mean that I speak about my own experience—particular, partial, limited, and therefore perhaps irrelevant to a large area of life, the area in which *you* live here at Oxford and there at home. Finally, it must mean that I cannot *prove* my case to you: that I cannot prove it at the deepest level when we shall be thinking about the existence of God or his nature; that

I cannot prove it at the level of everyday situations and confrontations, when we shall be thinking about such things as sex and ambition and vocation and hydrogen bombs and loneliness. I can only answer that, because the cause is so tremendous and the choice before you so desperately urgent, I must take risks. And I am much comforted by the fact that that is precisely what Jesus Christ told his closest friends to do. 'If you want to follow me,' he said, 'you had better forget all about security': whether the security of home life ('unless you hate your father and mother and brothers and sisters, don't come after me') or the security of a job ('look at the flowers . . . the birds . . . nature: and stop worrying about where your next meal is coming from') or, even, security from the tempest of passion and desire ('follow me . . . look at me . . . I offer you nothing in the way of comfort or ease or freedom from buffeting . . . I offer you a gallows, a total loss, failure . . .') The element of risk in the Christian religion is not something which passes away as one grows older, for it lies at the heart of the faith itself. A religion whose symbol is the cross is a religion which warns men off if they are timid about life—at least it ought to! Perhaps one of the reasons why it is necessary to have a mission in the University of Oxford is simply because that symbol, so evident everywhere on our buildings, has ceased to have reality and meaning as itself. Christianity has become, as we are so often nowadays reminded, part of the Establishment. And there is no room for a cross there!

But, to return to the main theme of these eight addresses, The True and Living God—the God, that is, who secures to man a changeless, unchanging, immutable standard by which all else can be judged and valued. The God, that is, who is operative *in* the world, not merely in the lives of men and women who believe in him, not merely in the institution called the Church, but in the whole of life. So that there is no single part of human experience which lies outside the range of his influence and power: so that all mankind's most glorious adventures, from reaching for the stars to probing for the origins of being, are his concern. The True and Living God! Standing over against the shadows which are taken for reality in our generation—power, affluence, prestige, at the personal and the international level. Standing over against the deadness which spreads through society when, as today, it yields to a view of itself based on materialism and determinism, a society of ants or formulæ. The True and Living God! The God, that is, to whom the vastness of the universe and the minuteness of the atom are standards of size without meaning: for to his infinity they are without comparison. Their truth, unlike his truth, being relative to the human mind which explores and measures them. And so the God whom man can know and adore, because in him is life.

I have expanded my title at length not because I want to pre-judge your own choice or your own consideration of the claims of Christianity, but simply to begin by making as clear as I can the reasons which led me to choose it. For it seems to me that if this week is to be of any use, it can only be so by presenting the issues straight and arguing them out. I come to you as a Christian. It would be ridiculous, and dishonest too, if I were to pretend to approach the contemporary world as one unaffected by that background and that conviction. It is my life. I have no other. But I hope you will believe that, just because I have been and am involved in this contemporary world with you, I share your problems and feel myself most intimately concerned with them.

Perhaps my only real justification for daring to undertake this series of addresses is that I have been rather closely involved with what is, after all, one of the major issues of our world: the rise of African nationalism and the tremendous challenge of race-relations. No one living and working in any part of Africa today can be outside the contemporary situation. He is involved, whether he likes it or not, whether he understands it or not, in one of the greatest revolutions of history. Moreover, he is bound, if he has any intelligence at all, to see that revolution against the broader perspective of world movements. Perhaps the danger is, for us who have the good luck to be in Africa today, to think too much in terms of our own vast continent. But at least it means we cannot go to sleep and forget the world itself.

I have come to you straight from Africa; from Tanganyika —the newest independent republic on earth. These addresses have been prepared as I walked about my diocese, an area the size of Wales, whose people are simple peasant farmers; where there is no industrial development at all, and, as yet, only the simplest form of agriculture. I have tried to think what I could say to you, while sitting in mud and thatch huts in the evening, under the stars of the great African sky. Could there really *be* any point of contact between that life and yours?

There was an evening in a little village called Huwe, not far from the great Ruvuma River. I had come there for the first time earlier in the day and been greeted by the whole village with true African hospitality and friendship. There were speeches and gifts of eggs and chickens, and there was a fascinating dance by masked dancers. In the evening, after supper, I sat outside my hut and the people gathered round in the moonlight to talk. Because I knew it would amuse them, I brought out my portable transistor set and tuned in to the news. What I heard was the voice of Major Gagarin, speaking from outer space: the voice of the first man to make that incredible adventure. And I could not begin to explain what it meant to the people sitting at my feet. Yet Gagarin and they and I were of the same world, of the same flesh.

The first, and most obvious, fact of our world is this great leap forward in scientific achievement and technological advance. A leap so vast, and so rapid, that mankind as a whole cannot adjust itself to it quickly enough. But it is a leap that has been taken. Man has no choice but to adjust. Inevitably such an achievement as the mastery of space-travel gives to mankind a new sense of power and of freedom. It opens a new dimension. There is apparently no limit, after all, to exploration and discovery. Yet, at the same time, we know that the very qualities and skills which make such advances possible also make possible the Bomb and the Balance of Terror in whose shadow we all live. It is a world of hope and of despair. Perhaps it has always been so. But today, because it is so inescapably one world, because we are so dependent upon one another, because we can know, within seconds, what is happening anywhere on earth and how it will affect us, we are more immediately conscious of this tension and of this paradox.

Yet I do not think, for Western civilization at least, that this is the most significant factor of our age. Surely that lies closer to the heart of man himself: to the way in which he thinks of life itself: of the environment which gives him the only answers there appear to be. More important than Einstein, for our generation, are Marx and Freud. It is they who have created the intellectual climate in which modern man lives and moves and has his being. And this is true for those who accept and believe—as I do myself—that each was making a vitally important break-through in the analysis of society and of the working of human nature, as for those who see only falsehood and evil in their discoveries. The consequence of what they discovered is, however, a world without freedom, a life without choice, an 'absurdity' in which man is always the victim of his environment or of heredity.

I try to keep abreast of what is going on in Europe by reading reviews of plays and novels: where possible by reading the novels themselves. And, inescapably, I get this impression of a civilization haunted by the sense that life is meaningless, a farce, a dirty joke. Perhaps this assessment is true for intellectuals only. But I think that the ordinary man, the ordinary undergraduate, is conscious of being the victim of forces only half understood: of movements of society over which there is no control: of his own unconscious to which, apparently, there is no access but which determines the course of his life and of his relationship with others. Whether by society or by the unconscious, life is determined: man is enslaved: there is no point in struggling to shape your own destiny: that has been decided. All you can do is to wait for Godot. And so, finally, ours is a world in which there appear to be no fixed standards of right and wrong any longer. Everything is relative, for everything has to be judged against this background of forces, social and personal, beyond man's control. So, internationally, truth becomes always secondary to expediency. It is less moral to observe an agreement than to move forward into greater power. So, individually, it is less moral to observe a promise '. . . till death us do part' than to find fulfilment with another, and part without recrimination.

In all I have been saying it may seem as if I take a very gloomy, very pessimistic view of the modern world. And perhaps it is that, living in Africa, and confronted day by day with simpler, more fundamental problems of human existence —what has to do with food and water and the development of natural resources—one feels a sense of loss for our Western civilizations. Certainly one gets pretty desperate at the thought that, inescapably, Africa is part of this world: is increasingly influenced by it: has her destiny linked to it whatever she may wish or will to do. But I think there is enough truth in what I have said for it to be recognizable. A world of hope and of despair: a world of forces against which the person struggles in vain: a world of shadows and unreality.

And over against this The True and Living God. Here is

the choice. We call him the Creator. We mean by this not that he made the universe at some point far away in time and left it to develop according to its own fixed laws. We mean, rather, that the whole Universe and everything within it, animate and inanimate, is dependent, has the quality (I cannot speak in philosophical language) of 'creatureliness': of developing or evolving in accordance with the will of its creator from moment to moment. We mean by this that individuality, the individuality of the sparrow as much as of the human being, is the direct concern of the Creator. We mean that every human discovery, in the cosmic dimension or elsewhere, is a discovery of some part of that creative process: is, in the truest sense, a gift from the Creator as well as a striving from the side of the Creature. And therefore we believe that man is made for adoration: and that without this he is inevitably and inescapably less than man. It is the acknowledgment of dependence, of creatureliness, that alone can make sense of the world: for this is the very first law of its being.

Without God, Marx and Freud are right. We have no freedom, we are slaves . . . 'for that we exchange the truth of God for a lie and worship and serve the Creature rather than the Creator . . .' and one must pay the price.

Of course, I cannot prove it to you. I can only try to describe it. I can only say 'Try and see.' And here again I am bound to be personal and to run the appalling risk of arrogance. I can only talk to you out of my own experience: it is all I have. There is such a danger of thinking that these words of mine about God, about the Creator, about his Creation, are all very well but have no relevance to contemporary issues—so why should they be relevant to me, in Oxford, today?

But you see, one inescapable consequence of thinking about God as Creator is the realization that he *cares*, and that his caring reaches across all the barriers of colour and race and tribe erected by man. And another consequence of this doctrine is that the caring is for each individual, attractive or unattractive: clever or stupid: rich or poor. And the most important consequence of all is that this Creature, by definition, belongs to and is made for his Creator. So that anything, or anyone, which interferes with his dignity as a person is in effect denying the sovereignty and purposes of God: is a blasphemer. When you are fighting against racial prejudice, or when you are striving to help forward a young country and its people, you need more than a theory, more than some good ideas. At least, I know I do. It is the knowledge, the certainty, that this is God's world, that these are his creatures, his children, his final purposes, that alone sustains me. Without it, I could see no point in anything that I have done or could do.

'We worship and adore the framer and former of the Universe; governor, disposer, keeper; him on whom all things depend; mind and spirit of the world; from whom all things spring; by whose spirit we live; the divine spirit diffused through all; God all-powerful; God always present; God above all other gods: thee we worship and adore.'

II. WHAT IS MAN?

Not long ago I was visiting a village in my diocese before the rains should come and make the road impassable. Like so many other places in the remote Southern region of Tanganyika, it is self-contained. That is to say, the villagers grow their own food, and in a bad year know what it is to be really hungry. Even in a good year, the diet is monotonous, the water has to be carefully used, meat is very much of a luxury. It is a wild and beautiful place: but the life of man can be precarious. And when sickness of any sort comes, it can be more than precarious, for the nearest clinic is a walk of twenty-five miles and the nearest doctor is nearly a hundred miles away.

The majority of people living in these parts of my diocese are, in fact, Muslim. But I had been to visit our Christian community, which is strong and vigorous. After the service, as always, the people came to talk and to bring their problems. One of them, a policeman, came to say that he had been urgently called home to the village (it had taken him a couple of days to get there) because his sister was desperately ill. Could I possibly take her to hospital on my way home? There had only been two or three cars in that village during the past six months: with the rains coming, there would be none: already she had been sick for two months and too weak to go the long journey to the clinic. She was, I understood, a Muslim. Of course, I agreed. But when I saw her, carried to the side of my Land-Rover in a litter, I saw nothing but skin and bones: it was far too late for that journey to hospital. Nevertheless I took her there, and she died a few hours after her arrival. But at least she died with whatever of medical and nursing skill we had at her disposal, and in a clean bed. . . .

I tell this story because it is so simple and so typical. It illustrates, of course, a good many things about emergent Africa which we could do well to think about. The fact, for instance, that in a developing country such as Tanganyika you are up against problems which lie far deeper than politics—in the ordinary sense of the word. It is food and water and soil to care for, and roads and bridges to travel, that are the real issues: 'political', if you understand by politics what concerns the ordering of human society. It illustrates, if I may dare to say so, one of the more disturbing features of life in England today. The fact that, while there appears to be a vast interest and concern for Africa, there is so little apparent fruit of this concern in the supply of doctors and medical services. As I address you now, I know that in the whole of Tanganyika there are fewer than three hundred doctors to serve the needs of over ten million people! Fewer than the staff of one of our London hospitals to meet the needs of a whole country! And half of the doctors there are supported by voluntary agencies, missionary societies, out of their very limited funds. It illustrates—or am I wrong in this?—the danger of arousing emotional concern for such issues as the colour bar and racial oppression: if such concern is just going to stop short at protests and boycotts and demonstrations and is prepared to give nothing in the way of service.

But I have used this story of an African woman dying in her village for another reason. Just because it is so typical, just because it can be repeated, is being repeated, a million times over and in a million different contexts, it poses the question I want to put to you tonight. What is man? What is man? It poses the question inescapably and in a form which we are all bound to recognize sooner or later. For if 'one event happens to us all': if sickness and death and the chances which bring them into our life are inevitable—why trouble to care for this one or that? How can the individual, the person, the dying woman lying there under the African sun, make any claim upon us? What—in fact—*is* man: more than the frame which gives him his shape, more than the flesh which, for such a short time, gives him an appearance of uniqueness, a beauty even, among creatures? What is *man*, more than one of an infinite variety of animals, who by evolution has acquired a supremacy, but who even in that supremacy is but 'a talking beast, and in his speech lies his reason.' What is man, if, when speech and reason fail, he has to be fed and washed and tended if he is to survive at all: dependent for every single need upon the accident of another's compassion?

The fact is that whatever view you take of the world, this is a question which poses itself and demands your answer. Whether consciously or not, you give that answer by what you do as much as by what you are. And in effect, the whole of behaviour in its human context *is* the answer. That is why in the modern world there is such a sense of bewilderment. What is man? And the Communist answers that man is the victim of economic forces which mould and form his whole life in all its complexities and that until those forces, by a dialectical process, are brought to their true use, man's life will be constantly frustrated and foiled. And the secular Humanist answers, if I understand him rightly, that until man can forget the irrational fears, the guilt, the grief and the cruelty which are called 'religion,' he will never grow up: he will go on trying to believe 'six impossible things before breakfast' and so will have no time for the service of his fellow men, the only service worthy of the name. And the Freudian answers that without self-awareness, without analysis, without that re-integration of the whole personality which is dependent on these things, man is incapable even of being man: he is a kind of living lie, unconscious of his unconscious, which *is* reality.

But, underlying all the answers (and there are so many more that I have left), it seems to me that in our world today there are two chief trends predominating and they contradict each other. There is that which takes away from man all significance: and there is that which gives him the only significance there is.

Our generation is overwhelmed by the vastness of the universe. Just because of the scientific break-through in our knowledge of this the littleness of our world has become a reality in an altogether different way from that of poetic imagery. As man stands poised to make the most fantastic adventure into space, he knows (he does not just imagine) the millions of 'worlds' 'out beyond the shining of the farthest star.' And what is man, against a background so vast? What is his little world? How can there be any great significance in it at all?

But it is not only vastness, it is Power that we in this generation have discovered. There is no need, here, to dwell on this, for it is this power of destruction available to man as a consequence of his own inventiveness which dominates all our thinking about relationships between countries, about the future of our own country, about the possibility of survival itself. Here is Power, different in kind from anything known before. And although it is dependent upon man's brain both for discovery and for use it overshadows human existence and threatens the very meaning of life itself. What is man— if in a second, under a mushroom cloud—he and his civilization and his future can disappear as if they had not been?

And it is not only Power that seems to knock away the foundations of human dignity for our generation. It is that sense of individual helplessness over against the impersonal machine-like quality of our civilization itself. The modern state, so complex, so increasingly dependent on what goes on in the dark 'corridors of power,' so uncontrollable and unaffected by the individuals who are its citizens; the very pace of communication, making reflection almost impossible, by which events in one part of the world have an immediate impact on another; automation; computers; 'Admass': all these symptoms, or perhaps even 'sacraments,' of our social order, pose the same question, all point to an answer along the same lines. What is man—if he is *part* of such a society as this? Is there any real place or meaning for the person, more than for the thing?

If I am right, it is because he feels himself so overwhelmed by vastness, by power, by technology, that man reacts into forms of self-assertion no less characteristic of this age than the forces themselves.

The greatest contrast between the Africa I know and the England I have come back to for this brief spell is not just a contrast between simplicity and complexity—though that is real enough. Nor is it a contrast between poverty and affluence—though that is horribly obvious at every level. Nor, even, is it a contrast between the vitality of a continent with the future to make and that of a continent struggling to break out of an inglorious past, though that too is a reality indeed. No. The greatest contrast, I think, between the Europe I read about and the Africa I know is in the matter of security. It is becoming a European obsession, whereas in Africa we can still live each day as it comes.

Security! To be safe! To have reassurance in a universe which is too vast and too full of power and too impersonal for comfort and ease of mind. How much one understands and shares it. But to hope to achieve this security simply by setting value on one's own possessions and accumulating more of them—this is a strange kind of error. Yet it is this which is so characteristic of our civilization today. It is this, apparently, which doubles the stream of emigrants to rich lands like Australia and South Africa, but leaves more under-developed countries to get poorer. What is man? If he is concerned with his own security above everything else he gives his own answer to that question: he is a slave. He has not even the elementary freedom of mastery over things. In East Africa 'things' are few and essential to life, and life therefore is what matters. It is not that Africans are necessarily *better* than Europeans: it is that in this respect at least they are *luckier*, though it is hard to know how long this simple state will last.

In the very process of trying to achieve security, of trying to make certain of self-hood, man achieves the opposite: not fulfilment, but diminution. Can it be that at a far deeper level the same thing is happening? This security which man longs for, and which he can never find in the accumulation of more and more 'things'—surely it must be found in relationships? I read the other day, in an intelligent article on sexual morality in England, the phrase 'Relationships between individuals are probably the last hope of this century. . . .' They have become so because the vastness of the universe increases man's loneliness, and the power unleashed increases his insecurity. And so, again putting himself in the centre of the picture, man hopes to find the answer—the peace, rather —in sexual gratification and fulfilment.

I recognize that I am middle-aged. I also know that there is a horrible danger of hypocrisy when those of one generation talk to those of another about sex and its meaning. I happen also to be celibate, having taken the vow of chastity when I joined a religious order twenty-two years ago. All this may put me, in your eyes, out of court. But that risk I shall have to take! I only ask you to believe me when I say that on this subject at least I know that I am human, nor would I dare to pretend to know all the answers. But there are three characteristics of the present situation which seem to me to be ominous, if not absolutely disastrous, for Western civilization: first the assumption that man is free in the sphere of sexuality because it is his personal and private concern; if indeed this assumption is true, then 'relationship is the last hope,' for there is nothing else upon which to base a sexual morality. In consequence of this it follows that (2) sexual morality is entirely relative: there can be no fixed moral standards, for this is a denial of individual freedom. And so we have (3) the separation of the sexual relationship from all other human relationships, and its use not as an expression of love which involves sacrifice (self-giving) but as an expression of desire which means self-gratification. There is a very real danger that in isolating sex and becoming obsessed with it to the exclusion of almost every other faculty, one's whole view of the nature and destiny of man will become false and off-balance.

What is man? Again, he is enslaved: not by things, but by himself; by the urgent passion of his own body and by the knowledge that it can never, of itself, find peace and satisfaction. Never—because this is not 'relationship' at all.

How, then, can man *be* significant in a world like this? He wants reassurance so desperately: he wants to escape the loneliness of his own situation. 'Our age,' says an American scholar of this University, 'has produced a new kind of eminence. This is as characteristic of our culture and our century as was the divinity of Greek gods in the sixth century B.C. or the chivalry of knights and courtly lovers in the middle ages. It has not yet driven heroism, sainthood or martyrdom completely out of our consciousness. But with every decade it overshadows them more. All older forms of greatness now survive only in the shadow of this new form. This new kind of eminence is *"celebrity."* The celebrity in the distinctive modern sense could not have existed in any earlier age. The celebrity is a person who is known for his well-known-ness. His qualities—or rather his lack of qualities—illustrate our peculiar problems. He is neither good nor bad, great nor petty. He is the human pseudo-event. He has been fabricated on purpose to gratify our exaggerated expectations of human greatness. . . . He is morally neutral. . . . He is made by all of us who willingly read about him, who like to see him on television, who buy recordings of his voice. . . .'

It is this 'image,' this new idol created by the fantastic power of modern mass-communication, it is this possibility of achieving fame without the intrinsic merit of fame, which is today the spur to so much of human ambition and endeavour.

What is man? More than ever before he is at the mercy of unreality. Truth itself, apparently, even the truth about man's own nature, is relative, is conditioned, is prefabricated and fitted to meet man's own longing for reassurance.

What is man? Over against the picture I have drawn—and perhaps it is in some ways a false and distorted picture—what does the Christian faith have to say?

The first thing to notice about Christianity is that, more than any other religion, far more than any philosophy, it is concerned about man. Secular humanism can never have an equal concern, for humanism does not believe, as the Christian must, that there is an eternal and infinite dignity in human nature itself. 'Let us make man in our own image, after our own likeness'—that is the stupendous claim. That man is made in the image and likeness of God his Creator. And it is this infinite and changeless dignity, belonging to human nature itself, which determines the Christian attitude to individuals and to societies. It is this which makes it impossible for the Christian to regard man as of less importance, less significance, than the State. It is this which makes discrimination on grounds of colour or race or creed not merely undesirable or inconvenient, but wrong. It is this which makes a leper or a thalidomide baby or a murderer equally the object of Christian concern.

If you read the Gospels objectively, it is surely Christ's *concern* with men and women *where they are*, that is its clearest and most startling feature. They said of him that he ate and drank with publicans (quislings) and sinners (prostitutes): and he said of himself that he wasn't interested in religious people. 'I came not to call the righteous, but sinners . . .' It is man he is concerned with. Whether as a blind beggar sitting in the dust by the roadside; whether as a learned doctor of the law coming to him by night: whether as a hireling tax-collector in his office: whether as a fisherman out all night on the lake or as a prostitute from the streets of Magdala or as a governor of a Roman province trying to find a way through his own dilemma of truth and falsehood.

He calls himself—it is his favourite way of describing himself—'The Son of Man.' For he has shared, from the cradle to the grave and beyond the grave, our human condition. Born in a wind-swept stable at Bethlehem: a displaced person, a refugee, in Egypt: a carpenter's son, learning a craft, experiencing the ordinary simple things of village life: alone, in a desert place, and 'tempted in all points like as we are'—feeling the full force of those storms and passions which are human nature: surrounded by crowds, sought after by sick in body and mind, criticized, rejected, denied, betrayed . . . The list is endless, for there is no human experience which is not there, shared from inside, known completely, made his own. Even the final experience: even death: even, apparently, the darker shadows which can surround that moment: 'My God, my God, why . . .?' 'The Son of Man'—this is he who for Christians is the expression of what man is meant to be; and the whole of human experience, he has made his own.

But the Christian faith also says of him that 'he emptied himself' in order to identify himself with our humanity. Or —in the words of the Christian creed—'he was made man.' He who is God of Gods and Lord of Lords lays aside the glory of his Godhead and clothes himself with the garments of human nature. As St John puts it, in describing the Last Supper: 'He laid aside his garments and took a towel (the mark of a slave) and girded himself and began to wash the disciples' feet.'

For man, though created in God's image and likeness, is in fact a creature: is dependent: is one who, because he is so created, can find meaning and purpose and freedom only in obedience to his creator. 'Creatureliness'—this is the mark of human life, the way to freedom.

And the Christian Gospel says one more thing about man— a thing so unique that it separates utterly the Christian faith from all others. Not only does man come from God. He goes to God. That same manhood, human nature itself, in which he clothes himself at Bethlehem is 'at the right hand of the Father'—is taken up 'unto God'—and therefore has a destiny, as well as an origin, in glory.

In glory. . . . 'In the beginning, God . . . In the end, God'—and in between, human history in all its richness and variety, its wonder and its tragedy, its splendour or its degradation.

'In the beginning, God . . . In the end, God'—and in between, the individual personal life in its changes and chances from the cradle to the grave, infancy, adolescence, maturity, senility.

'In the beginning, God . . . In the end, God'—and in

between, you and I, with our own choices to make for good or ill.

It is purpose, it is *meaning*, which the Christian faith claims to bring to human life. It is, if you like, the transforming of existence into life itself. The human condition is transformed and perfected not by man's own intelligence alone: not by the application of that intelligence alone either: but by faith.

III. THINGS

I have, I know, already indicated a little of the meaning of life in what is called an under-developed country like Tanganyika today. But I do not feel I have conveyed even a fraction of the sense of *reality* one has in living in a country which has not yet been submerged in industrial development, and where in consequence man is conscious all the time of his dependence upon creation.

I use the word 'creation' deliberately. It is becoming increasingly hard in this country, in Europe and America, to reach and find reality at the level of creation at all. Technology, mechanization, automation, make a screen between man and creatures. The child born in this age may get his food packaged, pre-cooked, frozen: milk out of a machine, vegetables out of a tin, water out of a tap, air out of a conditioner, warmth out of (perhaps) an atomic reactor.

All this is, of course, both familiar and inevitable in the kind of society which is 'developed.' I am only quoting it because I think it is important to recognize that it changes man's attitude to all those things upon which his life depends. I am not trying to advocate putting the clock back. I fully recognize the immense advantages of such a form of society. I have no wish whatever to be deprived of those advantages, for I enjoy them. But it is nevertheless true that the gulf between man and nature (however we are to define this) is wider today than it has ever been. And I think it is at least partly because of this gulf that we are confronted with our major world-problem—the problem of that other gulf between wealth and poverty as it affects nations.

Not long ago, in a village in my diocese, I was the witness of a scene which brought home to me most vividly one great truth about our world. Again, it is a very simple incident. It could be paralleled in countless parts of the world. It isn't at all exciting. I had arrived in the village, and, as is customary, the local head-man, or *mwenye*, came to greet me bearing a gift of eggs or a chicken—I forget which. Because he was so kind and so friendly, I asked him to show me his own home, and we set off together with a group of villagers down the hill. As we got close to a cluster of houses in the valley, I heard a great commotion and shouting, and I saw a youngster running away and others in full cry after him. By the time the *mwenye* and I had reached the bottom of the hill the boy had been caught, and, firmly held, he was brought to stand in front of us. He had been found washing in the stream which flowed along the valley—washing himself and his clothes in a place used by the whole community for drawing water to drink. He tried to excuse himself by saying he came from another village and did not know. He tried to escape the wrath of the *mwenye* by pointing to his torn shirt and accusing his captors of destroying his property. He put on a great show of anger. But in the end he had to submit to having his name written down, and in a few days' time he would stand in the local court and be formally tried for his offence.

Water, in Africa, can mean life itself. To be able to drink without fear of contamination—this is something essential to the whole community. To misuse water is therefore a grave offence. And ignorance is no excuse. *Water is sacred.*

This is what I mean when I say that we are nearer *reality*, in many ways, than you are. And we are nearer to it not just occasionally, but all the time.

In recent years, and increasingly I suppose with discussion about the Common Market, it has become obvious that—even more than the problem of survival—the greatest single issue confronting our generation is that of world inequalities: the plain fact that the vast majority of human beings are hungry, while the minority is affluent beyond all need. It is encouraging and stimulating to find in Britain such massive support for organizations like the Oxford Famine Relief Committee, and War on Want, and Food for the Hungry. It is good that, increasingly, we have become aware of our appalling failure in past years—especially in those lands over which we have had direct responsibility in government—to recognize, let alone to meet, the challenge. It is one of the signs of the whole movement towards world unity that at last we have begun to see the meaning of a population-explosion not just in terms of the land where it happens but as affecting the whole human race. But in all this there is the danger of recognizing the symptom rather than the disease. Here are vast reservoirs of wealth and productivity: draw on them for the needs of the famine lands of Asia and Africa. Or, here is a vast spiral of population increase, brought about by advancing medical skills: fewer babies dying, people living longer, diseases once endemic, like malaria or T.B., being brought under control: let us therefore control too the population, let us get a balance, a level, so as to curb not the hunger but the number of hungry mouths itself. Or—far more positively —let us bring all our skills to bear on productivity: on improving the soil and agricultural methods and the knowledge of nutrition. Let us train men from the countries themselves that are in need, so that they can return and serve their own people.

All these approaches are being made to this vast problem— though many people think it is too late. But none of them, nor all of them together, can reach the heart of the matter. For Wealth and Poverty, Affluence and Hunger, Abundance and Need, are not just the accidents of an uneven development of resources. They are, like everything else in a world which man organizes and controls, dependent upon the attitude of man himself. The root cause lies there in the human heart. And, just because it does so, Christianity—the faith that is concerned with man as man, and not just with modern man, claims the right to speak to this condition of the modern world.

There are three moments in the Gospel which have a peculiar and special relevance: an incident, and a parable, and an action. It is, it seems to me, upon these three moments that the Christian needs to dwell if he is to understand his own faith in respect of 'Things.' But it is even more important that this faith should be proclaimed in its integrity to a world that has lost its way, that is in mortal peril of disaster from the misuse or the forgetfulness of the meaning of creation.

The *incident* happened at a crossroads somewhere in Galilee. They had heard that he was coming—this strange new prophet from—of all places—Nazareth. There had been rumours in all the villages about the way a touch of his hand could bring healing, hearing, even sight to the blind. Men said that he spoke with a new kind of authority: as if what he said carried its own conviction apart from any appeal to the Law. There had been rumours of trouble too—between him and the authorities. It wasn't quite clear why the scribes and the Pharisees were against him in certain parts—but they had thrown him out of at least one synagogue. They said . . . they said . . . Well, now he was coming this way and they could see and hear him for themselves. So the crowd grew at the crossroads. And he came. An ordinary-looking man, if you ask me! But suddenly there was a movement in the crowd: a young man was pushing to the front—one they knew very well. His father was the richest man for miles around—had died recently, and this was his heir. And now he had got to the front he did a strange thing—knelt down in the road and looked up at this Jesus and said, so loud that everyone could hear, 'Good Master, what shall I do?

What shall I do to *live*?' A strange sort of question from one who had everything that life could offer. But it was a religious question really. Anyhow, it got that sort of answer. 'You know the Law. Don't kill, don't steal, don't fornicate . . . say your prayers, be honest, keep straight . . .' You could see the anger in the young man's face, and hear the bitterness in his voice. 'That stuff again! I tell you I've done all that—ever since I was a kid! I came to you because I'm not satisfied: because if that is what religion is, it means nothing to me: it doesn't connect. . . . What more can I do? What more can I do to get some reality into living?' 'Go. Give up everything you have and come with me.' Go. Give. Follow. 'And he went away sorrowful,' we are told, 'for he was very rich.'

A simple story. And, I suppose, a pretty familiar one. But can it mean anything outside the context in which it actually occurred? It *seems* to mean that the cost of Christian discipleship—for some people at any rate—is the total renunciation of material wealth and the total commitment to a way of life which will make unknown and unending demands. In the long history of Christendom, it has in fact meant this to thousands—not all so gloriously attractive as a Francis of Assisi, but all, in their own way, recognizing a true freedom and a true peace in voluntary poverty. But what can it mean to man as man: to me as me? It must at the very least mean this: That if I want to use things rightly I must recognize whom they belong to. 'He had great possessions'—'he was very rich'—but he did not recognize, in the one standing over him, their true owner and Lord. But there's another line in that story which gives us the clue we need for ourselves. 'Jesus, looking upon him, loved him' —but he let him go! This discipleship, this obedience, this renunciation—it is grounded upon freedom. For love is free or it is not love.

The *parable* can be briefer, for it is so familiar as to be part of the current coin of language itself. Dives and Lazarus. The rich man who 'fared sumptuously every day' and the beggar lying at his gate full of sores 'and the dogs came and licked his sores.' And the beggar died and went to Paradise and the rich man died and was buried. And then that description, so unpleasing to our generation, of Dives in a 'place of torment' seeing, afar off, Lazarus in Abraham's bosom. The plea—first for a drop of water to cool his tongue: then that his brethren may at least be warned—and both pleas refused because 'there is a great gulf fixed.' What had Dives done? Was he suffering simply because he had had good fortune in the world and Lazarus evil? Is it so simple a story as it appears? Isn't it really the eternal comment on the hardening of the human heart—not by deliberate evil, not by a drying-up of ordinary affection (he had five brothers of whom he was fond), not by a vicious misuse of wealth for selfish ends but—by *privilege* itself? He wasn't hard on Lazarus. He just hadn't noticed his existence as a *person*. The Affluent Society may be full of philanthropists. But it kills compassion. A world divided by affluence and need is a world in danger of being divided permanently—not because these countries which have wealth are in themselves evil, but because privilege creates its own barriers until at last 'there is a great gulf fixed.'

The *action* is recorded at greater length and in fuller detail than anything else in the Gospels. It is set in the context of the most solemn moment, a moment identified by the Jewish people with freedom itself—the freedom that God bestowed when he led them out of Egypt, 'out of the house of bondage.' In the context of the Passover meal, we are told, Jesus took bread and said 'This is my Body,' and likewise, after supper he took the cup of wine and said 'This is my blood.' . . . Do this—this very thing that I am doing—in remembrance of me. But in the fourth Gospel, that of

John the beloved disciple, instead of a record of these works we have another picture altogether. He laid aside his garments. He took a towel and a basin. And he took *water* and washed their feet. 'If I your Lord and Master have washed your feet, ye ought also to wash one another's feet.' Do this—this very thing that I am doing, in remembrance of me.

Bread. Wine. Water. The things of human existence: the things, moreover, which symbolize the whole of human wealth. It is these things which in our way of life have been covered over with layer upon layer of unreality, so that we cannot reach them, so that we cannot know them in themselves.

If we are to meet the crisis which divides the world—not the ideological crisis between East and West, but the far deeper crisis of which we have been thinking—then we have to discover an attitude to things, an attitude to the creation, which will give them a meaning beyond themselves. It is precisely this that the Christian faith claims to do.

'And God saw every *thing* that he had made, and behold, it was very good.' It is here that we must begin: in the truth that there is nothing in the whole vast range of creation that is bad in itself. So often the Christian seems to deny this. So often, to those outside the Christian Church, it is the fear of losing, by some prohibition or other, the good things of life, that is the most powerful deterrent. In reality it is the goodness of things as coming from the hands of a good Creator which provides the motive for using them with reverence. Christianity, as William Temple wrote, is the most materialistic of all the great religions because it asserts uncompromisingly that things—all things—are good.

But, at the same time, it is obvious enough that good things can be used for evil purposes. That, in fact, this is what man succeeds in doing from generation to generation. Until he is confronted with the kind of situation in which he finds himself today—his world divided, and divided at a moment in history when it could most easily be one. How do we recover our reverence for things? 'He took bread . . . he took the cup . . . he poured the water,' just as on the hillside in Galilee he took a few loaves and fishes and fed five thousand. Just as, on another occasion, he took dust of the earth and wet it and used the clay to give sight to the blind. Just as the hem of his garment, because it was his garment, gave healing to the woman who touched it from the midst of the crowd thronging him. . . .

We have to put things back into the hands of Christ—or rather, we have to receive them from the hands of Christ—if their meaning, their reality, is to be restored. There is no other way. But, of course, I cannot prove it to you. It must be your choice, not mine.

All I can say is that, when it is tried, it works. 'They had all *things* common.' That was the condition of Christianity in its first days. 'All things common'—not because of some vague idea that it would work better that way. Not, either, as a matter of individual choice which could be taken or left. They had all things common, for they knew themselves to *be* the Body of Christ. And so they knew also that only so, only by becoming his hands, his feet, his voice, could they proclaim his truth.

In his book *Love, Freedom and Society*, Middleton Murry had some very hard words to say about the Church: 'Christianity has lost the masses . . . but the Christianity which has lost the masses was and is . . . a Christianity compromised at innumerable points with the social and natural order. The emergence of a new social and natural order must compel a profound revolution in the Christian religion if it is to have any hope of regaining the masses. It will have, therefore, to become a religion of love between men. It will be said that

Christianity has always been this: but the claim on behalf of the historical, empirical, materialist Christian Church is untenable. It has condoned and even perpetrated every conceivable crime against love.'

Here is a statement and a point of view which may well find acceptance in this audience. The failure of the Church to live up to its own teachings in every generation—perhaps especially its apparent condonation of power and privilege.

In our divided world, no doubt, the awareness of wealth and poverty at the national level has grown to be the most obvious *moral* challenge to our generation. This is proved by the kind of response made to appeals by Oxfam, Freedom from Hunger, War on Want: by the creation of organizations within UNO to meet specific situations in the hungry lands, and by the magnificent work they do.

And it is assumed—I think pretty widely—that support for such magnificent organizations is the best kind of answer we can make to this moral challenge. God forbid that I should seem to question the need or even to the smallest degree lessen the support. For all that is being done and will be done I thank God.

But I want to remind you of one fact. I ask you to consider it as objectively and fairly as you can, and to draw your own conclusions. The division of the world is not a *new* thing: only the knowledge of it is new. Hunger, disease, poverty in Africa and Asia, affluence in Europe and America, are not the product of this generation. But when these things were hidden and obscured and out of sight—who cared? Who *in fact* cared—for the lepers and the blind and the sick and the hungry? Who *in fact* cared, that children should have schools, that the sick should have hospitals, that the old and the broken and the lonely should have homes?

This is a matter of history: not of legend. The proof of it is not in books, it is there, now, in being for you to see.

There would be no schools—there would be no hospitals—there would be, I dare to say it, no freedom—in Africa today, if it were not for those who, in the name of Christ and of his Church, saw where the challenge lay and went to meet it.

They knew—and the Church has always known—that *only* the hands of Christ can *truly* heal.

IV. EVIL

Two or three years ago I went to see that magnificent musical *West Side Story*, haunting and unforgettable for many reasons: a comment on so many of the human problems of our particular day. As you will of course remember, the theme of it is the rivalry between two gangs on West Side—a sort of modern *Romeo and Juliet* story, with the Montagues and Capulets transformed. And perhaps you also remember that moment, after the shooting by one gang of the leader of the other, how the thugs who have done the murder gather at their usual meeting place, a drugstore. And they sit there talking, boasting of what they've done. Until at last the old man who looks after the store can stand it no longer, and he suddenly flashes out at them in bitter anger, 'You know, you make this world lousy!' And then one of the young gangsters replies: 'We found it that way!' We found it that way.

'And God saw everything that he had made, and behold, it was very good.' What is it, then, what principle, has somehow entered into this scheme of things to make it 'lousy'? Or is it only our own approach to the world, our own deliberate misuse and mishandling of what is good in itself? Have we, in other words, 'found it that way' or *made* it that way? And if we haven't, who has? Sooner or later, like the gangsters in *West Side Story*, we come up against the mystery of Evil. In a sense the most central fact of human existence, just because the presence of evil in the world is an inescapable presence. The man who is unaware of it does not exist. The man who makes light of it is either a knave or a fool.

And so it is a question that we cannot avoid, if, as I hope we do, we want to think of Christianity in the context of real life.

But here I want to disclaim any ability to explain to you the *origin* of evil. I shall not even attempt to expound the different explanations put forward in Holy Scripture and forming the subject for theological debate all down the centuries. I shall not, because I know that I am not a sufficiently good theologian to deal with the issues clearly enough: nor am I a philosopher trained to disentangle the so many conflicting threads of argument about the reconciliation of a Love, which by definition is Almighty, and ills which, flowing from the principle of Evil, appear to be Unlimited. With Dr Farrer I agree that 'Evil commonly strikes us not as a problem, but as an outrage. Taken in the grip of misfortune, or appalled by the violence of malice, we cannot reason sanely about the balance of the world. Indeed, it is part of the problem of evil that its victim is rendered incapable of thought,' so 'we must recover the power of dispassionate vision; and . . . exercise it on the place held by evil, including our own trouble, in the whole scheme of things.' So tonight I shall confine myself to the discussion of evil as we find it, as we recognize it most commonly in our own world—which is also God's world, which is also 'very good.'

But although we shall approach it almost entirely in this 'existential' way, it is a help to recognize that in the Biblical account of the origin of evil there are in fact two doctrines —not contradictory, but not necessarily complementary either, though they are frequently used to implement each other. To quote Dr Farrer again: 'The devil is one thing, original sin is another. If we deplore the state of affairs' (if, that is, we find that the world *is* 'lousy') 'and are unwilling either to shoulder the blame ourselves or to saddle our Creator with it, we might shift it to our ancestors' back, or we might shift it to Satan's. . . . Satan initiates the calamity by his rebellion against God. Our ancestors fall victims to his temptation, and so hand us down our inheritance of sin and guilt. As for us, we are perverted or enfeebled by original sin, and therefore lie open to Satan, who still goes up and down as a lion, seeking whom he may devour.' The origin of evil lies either with Lucifer or with Adam. The nature of their sin is disobedience. Its consequences are deprivation, separation and death.

And here I propose to leave the question of origins, for, as I have already said, the arguments which follow from them are outside my range and there are plenty of theologians and Christian philosophers in Oxford who will, I am certain, be glad to expound them. I would only say one thing which appears to me to be obvious. If we take the Lucifer story as the fundamental source, then we *do* recognize the cosmic nature of evil. We see evil not simply in terms of human existence or human relationships: not necessarily even as a condition of life in this single, tiny world of ours. If the origin of evil lies outside time and space, outside human measurement and human experience, it must, it seems to me, be present amongst 'principalities and powers, the rulers of the darkness' not of this world only, but of the cosmos itself. It gives to evil a far wider dimension—not physically, of course, but spiritually, or, better, environmentally. It is easier to see some kind of dim reason for nations and races behaving to one another the way they do, if they are involved in an environment where evil is not only present but active, positive, personal. I think, too, that those of us whose privilege it is to live and work in Africa find it easier to accept the idea of Satan's intervention and power because witchcraft is a reality: because we (or let me say I) who come from the artificiality of a European 'milieu' are forced to recognize, often and often, our own terribly limited ability either to understand or to meet the particular evil that this generates. It is not fear alone which springs from witchcraft. It is fear grounded in an experience of evil.

If we emphasize the Adam story, on the other hand, as fundamental in explaining the origin of evil, it is easier to grasp and to understand those fruits of evil which seem to belong to heredity, to humanity, *as* humanity, to man as man: capable of rational choice, and certainly choosing wrong: capable of heavenly aspiration, and certainly grubbing in the dustbins and cesspits of earth: capable of love, but certainly preferring lust.

But now, without referring back to the origins of evil, let us think of it as *fact*. The world, as we know it, 'is lousy.' Not, of course, all the time. Not, if we are honest, even most of the time: for most of the time, as Rose Macaulay once wrote in *The Towers of Trebizond*, 'life for all its agonies of despair and loss and guilt, is exciting and beautiful, amusing and artful and endearing, full of liking and of love, at times a poem and a high adventure, at times noble and at times very gay: and whatever is to come after it, we shall not have this life again.' But if we 'exercise the power of dispassionate vision and exercise it on the place held by evil in the whole scheme of things' we shall perhaps come closer to an understanding of it as a mystery—'the mystery of iniquity' —of which the Bible speaks and which is in fact the central challenge to every religion, every philosophy and every ideology. As someone has written recently (Daniélou), 'If Evil were a problem that depended on man's goodwill for its solution, Christ need only have been a preacher and moral rearmament would have been the true expression of his will.' If Evil was such a problem, we might add, then certainly after so much energy by such great men of goodwill—a Buddha, a Mahomet, a Gandhi—surely now the problem should be solved. But it is a mystery: a mystery affecting every man born into the world. It is worth considering as it affects us here and now in our generation, at this point in time.

It is possible, of course, to illustrate evil in countless ways, all of them familiar. I am bound to use examples.

I am bound to use examples, but I shall try to draw them from what I conceive to be different levels of our human experience.

There is nothing evil in nationalism. I take this as my starting point simply because I happen to have been involved in the stupendous revolution of the African continent over the past twenty years. History has, literally, seen nothing like it: the emergence of new sovereign states over that vast sub-continent, at a pace and with a vigour that is un-paralleled. So tremendous is it that it is virtually impossible for a contemporary mind to grasp what is happening. In Europe, this all happened so long ago that we have forgotten about it. Some of us tend to see nationalism as a kind of immaturity, as a nuisance. Yet, there in Africa, the only force that really counts is the force of African nationalism: the force which creates nations, which tries to find meaning and purpose in 'Africanism,' which is, whether we like it or not, transforming the whole shape of events in our world.

The simple point I am making is that nationalism is a creative, positive, essential force. It makes nations, and therefore unifies people who have been divided by tribalism or language barriers or social customs. There is nothing evil, looking at it like this, in nationalism. And yet somehow, in the world we know, it can become so swiftly and so easily the instrument of some of the worst evils. Of war, for instance, when national aggressiveness is given free rein. Of tyranny within the nation: when national leadership is identified with the lust for power. Of racialism: when the nation identifies itself with a particular group based on colour or origin and sets out to eliminate the rest. Nationalism is not an evil. But the millions of graves scattered across Europe, and the streams of refugees and the silent gas-chambers of Belsen and Buchenwald and the ashes of Hiroshima or Dresden show what evil can *do* with national-ism.

There is obviously nothing evil in scientific adventure and discovery. It is, in fact, an almost perfect good, for it is a quest for Truth, and Truth is good—is, in Christian terms, God. It would be absurd even to dwell on such an obvious fact, with the evidence all about us in the field of medicine or psychiatry: in the incredible advances made to combat hunger and disease and to push back the frontiers of ignorance so that man can truly 'love life and see good days.' And yet . . . Our generation too has witnessed the use of such knowledge not only for total destruction in the positive source of the hydrogen bomb, but also in the control over men's minds: so that the distinctions of moral choice may be obliterated, so that truth may cease to exist as truth for the individual. So that man may be reduced to imbecility or animality. And your own knowledge and imagination can supply the rest.

There is nothing evil—so far as I can understand such things—in the use of a drug like thalidomide for the relief of pain and anxiety. Nor—God forbid the thought—is there anything evil in a limbless, eyeless deformity. But the *mystery* of evil is at work there in a way so obvious, so appalling, that one hardly knows how to think of it as part of a world that is 'very good.'

There is nothing evil—if we think of it objectively—in a

great spasm of the earth's cooling surface, or in a mighty wind, or in a tide sweeping across an ocean. But the ruins of a city shattered by an earthquake or blown to pieces by a hurricane or drowned in a tidal wave—that is another thing. Homelessness, hopelessness, naked pain—is there no evil here?

'And when the years have all passed' (I quote that magnificent passage again in Rose Macaulay's *The Towers of Trebizond*) 'there will gape the uncomfortable and unpredictable dark void of death, and into this I shall at last fall headlong, down and down and down, and the prospect of that fall, that uprooting, that rending apart of body and spirit, that taking off into so blank an unknown, drowns me in mortal fear and mortal grief.' For death, too, is the consequence of the mystery of evil: is, in fact, for each one of us, however we may escape the rest, 'the last enemy' and the inescapable one.

'We found it that way!' I have spent too long, perhaps, in illustration. But I have done so deliberately to emphasize that Evil *is* mysterious. And the Christian faith has always recognized this truth: has never claimed to explain it away as though it were a mirage or an imagining. There have been heretics, of course, from Arius to Mrs Baker Eddy, who have claimed to give the answer: to tear apart the curtains and the shrouds. But Christianity has never done so. The mystery of Evil, in the Christian Gospel, is confronted with that other mystery, the 'mysterium tremendum' of Golgotha and the Empty Tomb. I cannot, therefore, set before you any comfortable doctrine. I cannot give you, either your reason or your imagination, an answer that will make it possible for you to explain the 'why' of evil in all its manifoldness. But I can give you something else, something better than comfort, better than logic—I can give you a way of meeting the consequences of evil which will be sufficient to your needs. And I can do this, not because I dare to say 'I know,' but because I *have* to say 'I believe.' What I cannot do is to compel you to accept the way I give.

In the first place, 'God is Light, and in him is no darkness at all.' 'In the beginning God . . . In the end, God . . .' We must start there. We must start there because if God does *not* transcend Evil, utterly, completely, finally—there is no way at all. We are caught in an endless dualism between the powers of light and darkness, of good and evil. Creation itself is then inevitably seen as involved in an interminable struggle, and we, as creatures, are involved with it. God is perfect Joy, perfect Peace, perfect and unchanging Love, 'with whom is no variableness or shadow of turning.' And I am made for God and my heart is restless until it rest in him. These are not mere pieties, words to soothe and console. They are the words of revelation upon which the whole Christian faith rests. They are the words which make God to be God. 'Peace does not mean the end of all striving, Joy does not mean the drying of our tears; Peace is the power that comes to souls arriving Up to the Light where God himself appears.' It is God, transcendent and immutable and holy, who shows evil for what it is. He cannot be identified with it at any point if he is to save man from its power.

Then, 'He who knew no sin, *became* sin for us, that we might become the righteousness of God in him.' . . . It is in these words of absolute mystery and paradox that St Paul tries, stumblingly and haltingly, to express the mystery of God's identification with a world 'lying in darkness,' 'lying in the evil one.' God transcends evil. But God, at a certain moment in time, at a certain place, enters into history and becomes man: 'the Word,' eternal and immutable and dwelling in a glory which no man can approach unto, 'the

Word became flesh and dwelt among us.' The mystery of evil is still present in this world of space and time, is still present amongst principalities and powers. But God-in-man, he whom we call Christ, confronts it with the mystery of himself.

And it is he that we call 'Lord.' 'Ye call me Master and Lord and ye say well, *for so I am*.' The record of his life as we have it in the Gospels is, precisely, the record of his confrontation with the powers of evil. Nowhere does he recognize their authority. Everywhere does he meet them with the word of power. He is the Lord. So he stretches out his hand to heal the sick, to give sight to the blind and hearing to the deaf. For these things are not a part of God's plan and purpose for man—whether they originate with Lucifer or with Adam, they must be overcome. In his approach to human frailty, whether it is physical or mental or moral, there is never an instance in the whole of the Gospel which shows Christ *condoning* it as part of the human condition. Whether it be the leper or the paralytic or the prostitute— it is with words of power that he meets them. 'Go and sin no more. . . . I say unto thee Arise . . . take up thy bed and walk.' He is the Lord. And when they told him that Lazarus was dead, he wept. But not with helpless grief over the victory of that last enemy. 'Jesus said "Take away the stone." . . . "Did I not tell you that if you have faith you will see the glory of God." . . . Then he raised his voice in a great cry: "Lazarus, come forth." The dead man came out, his hands and feet swathed in linen bands, his face wrapped in a cloth. Jesus said, "Loose him and let him go."' He is the Lord.

He is the Lord. Transcendent; standing over against evil. But at the same time he enters into the human condition and shares it utterly. 'The word was made flesh.' In the

most familiar of his parables he spoke of a man on the road
from Jerusalem to Jericho who fell among thieves, and they
wounded him, leaving him half-dead. This is man. This is
man, the victim of the powers of evil. This is man in every
age, wounded, left alone to die in the ditch—the refugee,
the thalidomide baby, the Jew in the concentration camp,
and they pass by. We know the parable. I would remind you
simply of the phrase, used to describe the action of the
Samaritan—of the Samaritan who is also Christ, who is
also the Lord. 'When he came where he was, he went to
him. . . .' '*When he came where he was. . . .*' God in Christ
comes where we are. Into a world created 'very good,' but
now 'lying in the evil one': whether through Lucifer or
through Adam need not concern us.

The Christian Gospel is simply the proclamation of this
truth—not that the problem of evil is no problem, but that
he who is the Lord has come where we are, with power, to
overcome it.

> Men go to God when *they* are sore bestead
> Pray to him for succour, for his peace, for bread,
> For mercy for their sick, sinning or dead:
> All men do so, Christian and unbelieving.

> Men go to God when *he* is sore bestead,
> Find him poor and scorned, without shelter or bread,
> Whelmed under weight of the wicked, the weak, the dead:
> Christians stand by God in his hour of grieving.

> God goeth to every man when sore bestead
> Feedeth body and spirit with his bread,
> For Christians, heathens alike he hangeth dead:
> And both alike *forgiving*.

(Bonhoeffer—1944)

V. SIN AND FORGIVENESS

There was a series of articles recently in the *Sunday Times* about the present position in England with regard to marriage and divorce. The first article was called 'Morals in Confusion,' and it ended with these words: '. . . with the ideal of Christian marriage weakened by the spread of divorce it is easy for the alarmists to point to the 20 per cent of pregnant brides, the sixteen-year-old unmarried mother, as instances of a growing social depravity. But to be depraved one must deliberately break the rules. Today the rules *are not there*. . . .' 'Marriage has not decayed,' the article concludes, 'it has changed—to become primarily a human relationship with the emphasis on personal responsibility. . . . Relationships between individuals are probably the last hope of this century. But they can support a society only if they begin in self-knowledge and end in unselfishness.'

I was invited three years ago to attend a conference in London dealing with mental health and the vast problem of Guilt which shadows so much of society, both young and old, today, and which must be of concern to anyone who cares and is responsible, whether as a priest or as a teacher or a social worker. The chief speakers were a distinguished Christian philosopher and theologian trained in the School of St Thomas Aquinas, and the leading Freudian professor of this generation. Each read a paper. Each was obviously the master of his subject and was able to expound it most lucidly. Each was talking about the same subject—Guilt. But there was not a single point of meeting anywhere in the two addresses. It was not that they collided and disagreed.

It was just that they simply never met. There was no common ground. And the tragedy of this situation is that, to cure the ills of our generation, each needs the other. Without the Christian insistence upon a transcendent, all-holy God as the source of moral law, there is nothing but change and flux and purely relative values. 'The rules are not there.' Without some profounder understanding of human psyche (nature), and the new world of compassion it opens up, together with its penetrating analysis, it is only too easy to deepen the wound: to leave it open and unhealed.

So 'the guilt-haunted twentieth-century bewilderment' grows and spreads wider and even wider. It is caught with great clarity by Rose Macaulay (in *The Towers of Trebizond:* the speaker is not, of course, Rose Macaulay, but a character in the novel), quoted in the *Sunday Times* article I have been using as an introduction. I make no apology for quoting her again: 'That is what adultery is, a meanness and a stealing, a taking away from someone what should be theirs, a great selfishness, and surrounded and guarded by lies lest it should be found out. And out of this meanness and this selfishness and this lying flow love and joy and peace beyond anything that can be imagined. . . . And there is no way out of this dilemma that I know. . . .' 'No way out,' writes the commentator, 'human relationships are more valuable than rules.'

'The rules are not there' . . . 'human relationships are more valuable than rules' . . . 'Relationships between individuals are probably the last hope of this century.'

I have used this particular article at some length because it seems to me to illustrate supremely well and very accurately one of the great dilemmas of our generation. And I have used it because what the writer says in the context of an article about marriage, adultery and divorce applies to the whole field of what is called Morals today. The 'guilt-haunted twentieth-century bewilderment' may find its focus more certainly on problems of sexual morality than anywhere else. But in fact these problems are only a symptom of what is a far greater malaise, a malaise involving nations as well as persons, and groups within nations as well as individuals. For today 'The rules are not there.'

If the supreme virtue for a nation is that it should dominate all other nations and enforce its own ideology upon them, then truth and falsehood are equally valuable instruments for the purpose. There can be no trust, for there can be no truth.

If the supreme virtue for a group within a nation— management or trade union—is to secure for itself an absolute advantage in wealth and material benefits, then greed and covetousness are more valuable assets than the good of the community. There can be no fellowship, for there can be no rest.

If the supreme virtue for one member of a family is success, is to find 'room at the top,' then selfish ambition is in fact a more valuable quality than unselfish giving. There can be no family: for there can be no love to hold it together. What has happened to us that such a situation, such an atmosphere rather, should have come upon us?

'Human relationships are more valuable than rules,' they say. 'Relationships between individuals are probably the last hope of this century'—the last hope, and if it fails, what then?

The real truth is that Morality has broken down, 'the rules are not there,' not because we have suddenly discovered the *value* of human relationships, sexual, national or international, but because we have denied completely the fundamental relationship between man and his Maker, between the creature and his Creator, between ourselves, our country, our world, and the All-Holy, All-Knowing, All-Mighty One who is God of Gods and Lord of Lords. The real truth is that we have forgotten the meaning of *sin*.

Tonight I shall talk about Sin and Forgiveness. Assuming

a non-Christian audience, I recognize that even the words themselves have a kind of old-fashioned sound about them, as if I were talking to people who have grown out of the use of that sort of vocabulary. It is a measure of the change which has come upon our society. But I do beg you to believe that I recognize that no small part of the blame for this rests with the Christian Church itself—rests with such as I myself in the first place just because, so often, the Christian has *appeared* to identify sin with the enjoyment of God's creation. (Dancing, drinking, the true joys of human relationship between the sexes—to the outsider, even now, even with reason, these *appear* to be the very stuff which is condemned.) The revolt against the Christian attitude to natural good is in fact a miserable notion of what that attitude is. But it was, and is in my opinion, an error for which Christians must take a large part of the blame. But, at a deeper level than this I believe, the Church has to blame herself, because so often, and all through history up to this present moment, she has failed apparently to condemn great social evils: has even shared in the guilt of them: has even helped to initiate them in order to secure her position or to preserve it. The ghastly story of Christian persecution of Jews in country after country, and of failure, by and large, to protest against it effectively even in our own generation. Her equivocal attitude to war itself, and the scandal of Christian nations fighting one another. The horrors of religious wars—whether of Christians against Muslims or of Christians against one another in the same land. The silence in face of racial discrimination and the practice of it even in Christian communities, even at Christian altars. The acceptance by Christians of evil labour conditions and hunger and slum housing, and their refusal to recognize in an age of industrial revolution the emergence of class barriers so strong and so permanent as to destroy the very meaning of Christian community. The quiet arrogance of Christians when in positions of authority over men of different cultures and of different traditions: 'The heathen in his blindness bows down to wood and stone.' The attempt, made over and over again, to *enforce* belief or uniformity of behaviour in the name of Christ.

The list could be lengthened. . . . Nor is it enough to claim, as I know the Christian rightly can claim, that in spite of these colossal sins and failures a Christian civilization can still express mercy and truth and love more perfectly than any other. We have sinned. And by our sins and our condonation of the sins of others, we have estranged the brethren for whom, as we profess, Christ died.

Yet it is also true to add that the Christian is himself caught in a dilemma, and a stupendous one, in upholding moral standards by an appeal to Christian truth. For the plain fact is that, in our generation, scientific and technological advance has been so fantastic that it has thrown up *new* moral issues, involving *new* applications, and the Church has simply not had *time* to come to grips with them. Nor, I believe, has anybody else. The possibility of total nuclear war puts out of court all past discussion—even if such was ever valid— on the conditions for a Just War. There can be no such thing. But it also raises its own issues which are dividing Christians at this moment and to which, it seems to me, the Christian answer is still utterly confused. The sinfulness of nuclear war, or of the use of one single nuclear weapon upon innocent people, is not in question. Its inevitability is.

The population explosion: the vast issue of a rising birthrate and a falling death-rate in the very countries where food is scarcest and poverty greatest. This is a new problem: the direct consequence of new and precious discoveries by man. But the answer—the moral answer—is not so clear. The sinfulness of letting millions die of starvation in a world of plenty is not in doubt. The remedy of abortion or massive education in contraception is.

And there are the new worlds opening up to us in space, and the use of space itself and the spending of vast billions when our own world is still underfed and underdeveloped. There is the problem of the control of the human mind by drug or manipulation.

All these are *new* moral issues. All carry with them the alternatives of sin and righteousness. But all are so complex and so novel that the Christian cannot be blamed if he does not give an answer immediately—or if, as happens in fact, his answers are conflicting, muddled and obscure.

In the Africa I have known for nearly twenty years—both the complicated, fast-moving heartbreak of a Johannesburg slum and the simple, slow, infinitely hopeful land where my diocese lies in the South of Tanganyika—I have been looking after *people*—not *problems*. The difference between them and you, perhaps, is that they know what sin is and we Europeans have forgotten or explained it away. I have been looking after people: individuals. . . . Which is just another way of saying that I, a sinner myself, have had 'the cure of souls'— the unspeakable privilege, which belongs to the minister of Christ in a unique way, of caring for his flock. 'Be to them a shepherd—not a wolf,' I was charged on the day of my consecration as Bishop of Masasi—a shepherd whose 'sheep hear his voice,' who 'calls his own sheep by name, and leads them,' who 'when he has brought them out . . . goes ahead and the sheep follow, because they know his voice.' A shepherd, who alone can say of his flock 'I know my own sheep and my sheep know me.' And the thing I know best about them—because it is also the thing I know best about myself—is their sins. Does this sound quite horribly impertinent, even arrogant? If it does, I beg you to remember that the Master I try to serve and whose example as a shepherd I am pledged to follow as best I may was only interested in sinners. He had no time for anyone else—or so he said. For 'I am come not to call the righteous, but sinners . . .' This is the condition of Christian discipleship: recognition of sin.

I have been looking after sinners for twenty years and more. And if you have done that, you begin to know something about the nature of sin itself. Of course, it reaches you in as many different forms as there are people, as there are moods, as there are climates and customs and cultures. But the lie of an African schoolboy who is afraid of getting into trouble is a *lie*, like yours of yesterday. And the anger of an African woman with her lazy son or her drunken husband is an anger like that which made you quarrel last week with your girl friend. And the thieving of an African postman from the savings-bank he has to administer is no different from the stealing of those books you needed so badly and which were too temptingly displayed on Blackwell's counter. . . .

Sin: lies, anger, dishonesty, greed, adultery, coveting, sloth . . . and all of it so much a part of the whole of life: the frailty of life—the quality about life which drives you out in love and caring, because you know yourself: because you know that this liar, this thief, this adulterer, is *you*, and you depend upon a mercy and an understanding if you are to go on at all. You have to be a shepherd—not a wolf—because you not only 'know your sheep,' you know yourself as one of them. But you do also know Sin, Sin in itself. Sin for what it is—the spoiler, the betrayer, the destroyer of all that loveliness you are there to guard.

Well—what is sin? I cannot avoid a Christian definition: a Biblical definition. There are at least three ways, in the Christian dictionary, of describing it. All equally valuable: all complementary and building up its true meaning. In the Psalms we sing there are three words: 'transgression,' 'sin,' 'iniquity'—each in fact translating a different Hebrew word, and each carrying a different element of meaning. For 'transgression' literally means 'rebellion'—the expression of self-hood in opposition to the claims of God. And 'sin' means 'missing the mark'—losing the way, mistaking the direction of life as God means it to be lived. And 'iniquity' here means 'crookedness,' the effect of a turning-in upon self, of a false scent, of a deliberate choosing away from God's choice, God's plan of love.

Rebellion—loss—spoiling. This is sin. And you will already have realized that the word has no meaning apart from God. It is no good imagining sin in the context of purely human relationships—desperately as sin undermines and destroys those relationships themselves. It is no use imagining sin in the context of 'breaking rules' unless you can recognize behind the rules, the Ruler against whom you rebel. Sin—in its true and Christian sense, is *always* personal: the personal act of the creature in the presence of his Creator; or—better and truer—the personal act of the son in the presence of his father. Of the son who 'said to his father, Father give me my share of the property' (*independence*) and who when he had got it 'turned it into cash and left home.' Chose deliberately, that is, his own way of life apart from God. And found himself 'in a far country,' for having asserted himself, he had missed the way and was lost and alone with his self-hood. But not only alone: famished, so that 'he would have been glad to fill his belly with the pods that the pigs were eating: and none gave him anything,' for they knew neither the son nor his father in those parts. It was a personal choice. It carried him to a far country, to loss, to hunger, to an utter loneliness. But he is still his father's son. And when he came to himself he said, 'I will arise and go to my Father, and say to him, Father I have sinned—against God, and against you; I am no longer fit to be called your son.'

'Father, I have sinned.' How many thousands of times have I heard, I God's minister, I Christ's shepherd, I a sinner, those words from the lips of men. 'Yes. I have sinned.'

That lie was a lie—not a slip of the tongue, not a manner of speaking, not a way of being polite—but a lie. A choice of falsehood rather than truth. Done in the presence of God who is truth and who is all-knowing. It was a rebellion and a despoiling and a loss. And it was I myself who chose it. And that fornication was an act of lust, deliberately made, deliberately enjoyed, deliberately used for my own gratification. It was not done on behalf of the other, to console or comfort or to express my love and caring. I have sinned. For it was not only the other that I used for my pleasure, it was one made in the image and likeness of God, and it was in his presence that I made my choice of lust rather than love. 'Father, I have sinned'—for that sloth was sloth, not weariness or worry or anxiety, which made the long years slip by without mention of your name, without thought of your claims upon me, without one single word of thanks, of greeting even, from morning until night.

Of course it isn't expressed like that in Africa. But behind the simple words, that is the truth of it. Sin as sin. Acknowledged and confessed for what it is. Rebellion. Loss. Spoiling.

Have you noticed, in the Gospels, the precise moment when the opposition to Jesus crystallizes and becomes impregnable? The moment, that is, when once and for all he challenges the Law and proclaims the Gospel? It is in Capernaum, 'his own city,' and they bring him 'a man sick of the palsy, lying on a bed: and Jesus said . . . "Son. Be of good cheer; thy sins are forgiven." And behold, certain of the scribes said within themselves, "This man blasphemeth. . . . Who can forgive sins, save God alone?" ' This is the moment when the Son of Man claims divine authority—the moment, one might say, for which he had come into the world: to forgive sin. And those who were gathered round 'were afraid and glorified God which had given such power unto men.'

To forgive sin. To restore the rebellious will of mankind by a will of perfect obedience, freely offered. To make up the loss and the spoiling of mankind by sharing its consequences to the uttermost and transforming them. To say 'It is finished' only when, by that perfect offering of a perfect obedience, man is brought home again to his Father's house. 'I have finished the work that you gave me to do.' It is accomplished. It is complete. It is perfect. But it is still for man to accept forgiveness on these terms.

One of our greatest difficulties as men, as creatures with the limitations of 'creatureliness,' is to recognize how vast is the difference between God's attitude to the penitent and our own attitude to those who have injured us. 'When he was yet *a great way off* his Father saw him.' . . . There was no waiting for apology or restitution, no bargaining over rights or injuries, no demand for abasement and humiliation. Rather, 'he *ran* and fell on his neck and kissed him.' In George Herbert's words:

> Love bade me welcome; yet my soul drew back,
> Guilty of dust and sin.
> But quick-eyed love, observing me grow slack
> From my first entrance in
> Drew *nearer* to me. . . .

The initiative, even in penitence, perhaps especially in penitence, is always from God to man. If we forget this, then even our penitence can be pride.

And it is so easy to forget when thinking of penitence, and its most perfect expression in the parable of the Prodigal Son, that there was also an Elder Brother; that in fact the whole story is set in the context of that Elder Brother's attitude.

In some ways it is only too easy to recognize oneself as the prodigal. At so many moments in life one has had experience of the 'far country,' of the loneliness that is part of that country, and of the gnawing hunger for home which forces the cry, 'Father, I have sinned. . . .'

But man is also the Elder Brother, and frequently more recognizably so, as he returns along the familiar path under the stars to his home: as he returns to all that he has grown up with, to all that he is accustomed to and takes for granted in his Father's house. And because, on this occasion, it is no longer familiar: because he sees lights in the windows and hears the sound of music and dancing, he is 'angry and will not go in.'

What is God's attitude to rebellion and stubbornness? What is God's attitude to man when he refuses utterly to recognize anything but his own worth, his own abilities, his own integrity?

The Father in the parable, who is also the Father to whom we are bidden to pray, says to this unattractive boy of his the most stupendous words in the whole Gospel: 'Son, thou art ever with me: all that I have is thine. . . .'

And just because this particular parable lies at the very hearts of the Gospel where sin and forgiveness must also lie, it is the interpretation of that moment in the Gospel where sin and forgiveness meet in every act.

'Father, forgive them, for they know not what they do'— and as he cries these words, he looks out upon all the prodigals and all the elder brothers to the end of time. We are amongst them: we are there!

VI. JESUS CHRIST

While I was preparing for this week with you in Oxford, I read as many books as I could get hold of which I thought might be relevant to the contemporary situation in England. Indeed my great fear has been lest, being so far away and living under such different conditions, I might be quite hopelessly out of touch.

One of the books which seemed to me important from this point of view was Mr Aldous Huxley's *Island*. The reviews told me that this book was an attempt to 'frame an ideal': to answer the question as to 'what would be the character of a liberty-loving society dedicated to the proposition that its members ought to be helped . . . to realize their desirable potentialities.' In fact, *Island* is a Utopia, taking into account the particular problems of our day and generation: and not the problems only—the opportunities opened up by advancing knowledge in all fields of life.

So I read the book. It did not surprise me, of course, to find that it was a very violent attack on revealed religion and on Christianity in particular. Nor did it surprise me to learn that on the island which is Mr Huxley's Utopia missionaries are prohibited immigrants! But what did surprise me was what I can only honestly describe as the old-fashioned attitude to our generation which permeates the whole book. As if, in fact, we were still living in 1930, or even 1920, beset with the problems of a disillusioned post-World-War-I generation instead of our own. And, with regard to religion, this seems to me to be more evident than in other fields. Listen, for instance, to this bit of dialogue which occurs in the second chapter and which is spoken between the hero—Will Farnaby—and one of the children of the island. Will is coming back to consciousness after a fall from a cliff: the child has never seen him before.

'With a reassuring word, the girl halted, well out of danger, and held up the fruit. "Do you want it?" she asked. Still trembling, Will Farnaby stretched out his hand. Very cautiously she edged forward, then halted again and, crouching down, peered at him intently. "Quick," he said, in an agony of impatience. But the little girl was taking no chances. . . . "For God's sake," he implored. "God?" the child repeated with sudden interest. "Which God?" she asked. "There are such a lot of them." "Any damned God you like," he answered impatiently. "I don't really like any of them," she answered.' And, later on, in chapter five, an extract from the works of the Island's chief reformer: ' "In religion all words are dirty words. Anybody who gets eloquent about Buddha, or God, or Christ, ought to have his mouth washed out with carbolic soap." ' And there is much more in the same strain.

Now it seems to me, apart altogether from whether one agrees or not with Mr Huxley's views on religion, they simply are not relevant to our world. Man, today, is *not* tormented by having to choose between so many Gods. He thinks that God is dead. Man, today, is not in great danger of becoming hypnotized by those who get eloquent about Buddha or God or Christ. He is far more likely to be aroused by C.N.D. or the peril of Communism.

Of course I know that my own experience is horribly limited. But at least it does embrace life on one of the most vital continents in the world, the continent of Africa in its revolutionary phase. And on that continent there are diverse religions—all of them ancient, all of them rooted in the very soil of the continent. Because I am not anything more than an amateur, I know how dangerous it is to generalize about such a vast and intricate subject as the comparison of religions. But one thing seems to me to be so self-evident that I can risk saying it. It is that in Africa today the religions which matter are in fact only three—Islam, Animism and Christianity. And influencing all three directly or indirectly is the overwhelmingly powerful force of African nationalism—capable of becoming a religion itself—already, in many parts of the continent, channelling away the energy and drive and enthusiasm of the young from the old faiths into this new and thrilling and all-absorbing activity of nation-building. But of 'many gods' competing for the heart of Africa there is no sign whatever.

And if my very superficial knowledge of Europe is at all correct, the situation here is even simpler. I would like to read to you a brief quotation—because it appears to me so deeply prophetic—from the *Letters and Papers of Dietrich Bonhoeffer*, written eighteen years ago from the German prison a year before he was executed. 'The movement beginning about the thirteenth century,' he wrote, 'towards the autonomy of man (under which head I place the discovery of the laws by which the world lives and manages in science, social and political affairs, art, ethics and *religion*), has in our time reached a certain completion. Man has learned to cope with all questions of importance *without regard to God* as a working hypothesis. In questions concerning science, art, and even ethics, this has become an understood thing which one scarcely dares to fret at any more. But for the last hundred years or so it has been increasingly true of religious questions also. . . . As in the scientific field, so in human affairs generally, what we call "*God*" is being more and more edged out of life, losing more and more ground. . . .'

Bonhoeffer goes on to develop his special theme of a

'religionless Christianity' as the answer to a world which has 'come of age'—and of this I shall not attempt to speak or to judge. The only point I wish to make is that, so it seems to me, Mr Aldous Huxley is fantastically wrong in thinking that the issue is that of a vast and varied pantheon of gods to choose from. The issue is that God is 'edged out of life'—in other words, to this generation, dead.

This is not true of Africa. God is still God—the Sovereign head of Life. And because he is so, the relationship between the Animist and the Muslim and the Christian is a reality: is, in the religious context, *the* reality of this moment in African history. I suppose one of the greatest single movements in the story of religion is taking place today in Africa and Asia, as a direct consequence of the end of colonialism and the era of European domination. For the first time for a century the Christian faith can be itself—a faith, and not a culture supported by external forces of administration and education and law. But, far more significant than this, there has been a revolutionary change in the whole approach to the other religions, of Islam and Animism, which is still only at its beginnings, but which opens up a new era of quite literally infinite possibilities. It is grounded in three new factors—all equally important.

First, there is a break-through in knowledge and understanding of other faiths—the result of a vast scholarship in which the anthropologist as well as the missionary has played a part. Secondly, there is a new humility, a sort of penitential humility, on the part of Christians for their own blindness and arrogance in the past; for their mistakes and misunderstandings and their misdirected zeal. I live in a part of East Africa where Islam has been strong and vigorous for seven hundred years—particularly along the coast. The site of Kilwa, one of the greatest and most ancient sultanates in

Africa (tenth to twelfth century), is in my own diocese. In very many of my elementary schools—perhaps in most— there is a great majority of Muslim children. When we celebrated Republic Day on December 9th last year, the prayers for God's blessing upon our nation were said by the local Sheikh and by myself. The President of Tanganyika, Dr Julius Nyerere, is a Christian: his Vice-President is a Muslim. We know, in Tanganyika, that without humility, without courtesy, without love, we cannot commend the faith that we hold as a faith grounded in those very qualities. Perhaps I cannot express this new approach better than in the words of Victor Gollancz, in his preface to *The God of a Hundred Names:* 'From amidst diversified and often warring creeds: over a vast span of history: in the language of many a tribe and many a nation: out of the mouths of the learned and simple, the lowly and great: despite oceans of bloodshed, and torturing inhumanities, and persecutions unspeakable— the single voice of a greater Humanity rises confidently to heaven saying, "We adore Thee, who art One and who art Love: and it is in unity and love that we would live together, doing Thy will." '

But those of us who live and work in Africa as Christians, entrusted with the particular and fearful task of guarding the flock of Christ and protecting it from error, know only too well, also, the extent of the gulf which separates one wor- shipper from another. We do not imagine—in a divided world—that we alone can bring unity, nor even that we have achieved anything: we have but begun. But at a deeper level than all this, the Christian Church in Africa has for many years gone much farther in the real understanding of her mission than is often recognized. Again I can speak only out of my own experience—out of the day-to-day experience in a country diocese, virtually cut off from the capital for half the year—an Africa that is typical of the most con- servative forces, the peasantry, the small farmer, the generation breaking away from illiteracy, but only just. To know a people's language, so that you can truly share their thoughts: this is the first step in identification with their life. From the very beginning this has been our rule. Quite a costly one, when, like me, you are middle-aged before you begin! To love the simplicities of life and to share them too—so that you erect no barriers of wealth or comfort or privilege: the curse of European Christianity in South Africa and Rhodesia. This too, we have tried to express in our simple buildings, our mud and stick churches, our standard of living. To recognize what is good and worthy in so much of African culture and tradition and to include and incorporate rather than to destroy it. So, for years, the initiation rites of our people have been recognized as precious and valuable parts of the whole social fabric, as being wholly consonant with the mind and teaching of Christ. But even so, we have failed. We have failed because, by and large, we have still left outside so much of the rich culture of Africa—music and dancing and form—which could have made the Christian Church less alien and strange than it is. We are learning— even if so late—that the treasures of our Christian culture are not made brighter by being locked up in the cupboard of Western civilization: that they glow and glisten better, and are enriched most wonderfully, when they are taken into African hands.

Yet, having said all this, I have left the most important thing unsaid. Whether to Africa or to Europe: whether to those for whom God is a reality or to those for whom he is a myth: whether to the learned or to the simple—the Christian *must* proclaim, whatever men may say or do to him for acting so, the absolute uniqueness of his Faith. For this is not his own claim, worked out, or worked up, against the claims of other religions. It is *there*. It is the *Gospel: good news*. Without this uniqueness, the Gospel itself is meaningless and empty. Without it, indeed, there can be no Gospel, no 'good news,' at all. But in what does this uniqueness consist? Again, I beg you to believe that this is a *real* question to me—and, I think, to anyone who has the responsibility of working within the Christian Church in Africa today. How would I dare to go there—how would I dare to stay and be identified with Tanganyika—if I knew that the foundation of all I said and did was a lie? For often, when my own people come to me in trouble—over a marriage, over disease and sickness, over death—I have to clothe myself with the authority of my master in order to answer them: in order to maintain the difference between truth and falsehood: in order to assert the uniqueness of him whose servants we are. 'In Christ, God was reconciling the world to himself.' This 'is the revolutionary fact which has turned all human ideas about God and man upside down' . . . this . . . 'is the essence of the Christian Gospel . . . it is a tremendous fact, reversing all ordinary values including especially the values of religion. . . . Christianity alone of all the great religions asserts these staggering truths about the God it proclaims.' First—that he is *Personal:* secondly, that he *acts* in history: finally, that he *loves* mankind so supremely that he identifies himself with them in order to reconcile them to himself. 'He loved them *EIS TELOS*, to the end, to the uttermost.'

He is *Personal*—not the Absolute, not the Unknowable, not the One, of Hindu or Buddhist (or Muslim) thought— but Personal. It is this very fact which gives the Bible also its uniqueness as the Word of God, the Revelation of God. For he—not an idea, not a system—but he, the Living God, shows himself to a particular human people in a particular moment of their history (a long moment by our standards, maybe) and says 'I am.' And it is through the lips of those he has chosen, from within the people he has chosen, that the knowledge of him is made known, deepened, filled out. Through an Abraham, a Moses, a Joshua, a David—because, knowing him as a Person, and only so, they can lead and guide their people along the path of their destiny. Nothing less than the experience of God as personal could explain their steadfastness in times of disaster: their patience and courage in face of rebellion: their 'faithfulness,' to use a Biblical word, when all the world around them is a howling wilderness or the march of armies bent on their destruction. God is known, is revealed, is spoken to—*as if he were a man!*

And yet, that is the one thing, in the Old Testament, that we know he cannot be. It is the stupendous paradox of those immensely varied writings, coming from different pens in different generations, that this God with whom his servants speak face to face—is yet always 'the High and Holy One, who habiteth Eternity', the God whose very name no man may utter. 'Thus saith the Lord,' say his servants the prophets. It is the source, the only source, of their authority. And it is enough. It is enough, in confrontation with the kings and rulers of the earth when their message is a message of doom and destruction: it is enough also when that doom has come and that destruction has destroyed and only a remnant is left, scattered and spoiled 'in a strange land' to hear them. 'Thus saith the *Lord*.' He is the Living God. Personal. Reaching his people with words of life so strong and meaningful that, throughout the centuries, they must hear.

But he is also the God of History. And in this too he is unique. He does not only teach his people—taking and using men for this purpose. He is *with* his people. . . . 'He taketh the simple out of the dust, and lifteth the poor out of the mire.' The Old Testament is the story of God intervening in history: *using* history. It is this or it is nothing. Covenant, Exodus, Prophecy itself—this is God 'the ruler of all history, using Israel as a messenger to make him known to all nations

. . . the theme is the sovereignty of God, shown in a particular history,' but 'to be realized in a climax which will affect *all* history.'

And the climax is the Person of Jesus Christ, the Lord. This is our Faith. This is its uniqueness. This it is which distinguishes it utterly from all other faiths, philosophies and religions. It is in Jesus that men are confronted with the Living God. 'No one has ever seen God: but God's only Son, he who is nearest to the Father's heart, he has made him known.' 'Anyone who has seen me, has seen the Father.' This is the challenge of Christianity to every age, and to every nation under heaven. There is no other. And this is the only valid and justifiable reason for people like myself going to Africa to live and—I hope—to die there. It is also the only reason why I stand here in front of you tonight.

'In Christ, God was reconciling the world to himself.' That is the briefest, and also the most perfect, statement of what is called, in theological language, the Atonement: the making at-one of the human race and its Creator. And, just as I have tried to avoid theological language in these addresses, so also I would avoid discussion of the different explanations of how that at-oneness was achieved. God—in Christ—reconciling the world to himself. Or, if you prefer it, 'There was none other good enough to pay the price of sin, he *only* could unlock the gate of heaven and let us in.' By turning all human ideas about God and man upside down, until this revolution finds its extreme expression there upon Calvary. 'Father, forgive them, for they know not what they do. . . .' It is all one with that love which in Galilee, by the lakeside, in Capernaum, in the market place or the synagogue, or the home, reached out to man 'where he was' and said 'Go in peace, thy sins are forgiven thee.'

'My God, my God, *why* . . .?' It is all one with that love which, in the desert or in Gethsemane, or when his enemies gathered to plan and plot against him, reached out to a world 'lying in darkness' to a world when 'it was night.'

'It is finished. . . .' And so, too, it is all one with a love for man which is indeed triumphantly complete and perfect, embracing the publican and sinner, the prostitute and the infidel, the crazy, the blind, the rotting corpse in the tomb. 'In his life and death alike' (writes Dr Lampe) 'God was acting towards sinners, breaking through their self-centred resistance and reconciling them to himself. His suffering and death are the climax of man's attempt to justify himself in hatred towards the God whom he fails to recognize as such, to rid himself of his sense of guilt, which is both a symptom and a form of his self-justification, by killing the one who spoke and acted in God's name. . . . The Cross is the ultimate sign of man's hatred; and in that very focal point of hatred the love of God accepts him despite the worst that he can do, in his most extreme sinfulness and bitter enmity. . . . It is the paradox and miracle of love, whose triumph, and with it man's reconciliation, is sealed in the Resurrection.'[1] Christ—The True and Living God.

But, of course, I cannot prove any of it to you. I cannot prove it any more than the empty tomb and the crumpled grave-clothes proved to John (his friend) that Jesus was risen from the dead. 'He saw, and believed.'

I cannot prove it any more than the figure of a gardener, moving in the half-light of that first Easter morning, proved to Mary of Magdala that the body had not been stolen from the sepulchre. 'Jesus said to her, "Mary!" She turned to him and said, "Rabboni . . . Master." '

I cannot prove it any more than the words of ten frightened men, gathered behind locked doors when he suddenly 'came and stood among them' convinced Thomas that his agony of doubt and despair was ended. 'Then he said to Thomas "Reach your finger here: see my hands; reach your hand here

[1] *Soundings*: 'Atonement': pp. 190-1.

and put it into my side" . . . and Thomas said "My Lord and my God." '

No. I cannot prove it. There are no words of mine sufficient for the mystery of God made man—of God the reconciler, living, working, saving in the world which is such 'a far country' and yet his own creation. For Love itself—even divine and infinite and perfect Love—cannot compel.

'Jesus, looking upon him, loved him.' But he let him go!

VII. THE CHURCH

'When we pronounce the word "Church," ' writes Giovanni Miegge, 'we think immediately of that majestic—and highly ambiguous—organism which has played so central a part in the history of the past twenty centuries. It depends on our point of view whether what comes first to our minds is the mighty organization of the Roman Catholic Church, with its hierarchy, its priesthood, its orders of monks, its laity organized for action, its social doctrine; or the Evangelical Churches in all their manifold variety, with their splendour and their shame, their agreements and their disagreements, their flexible theology worked out in so many varying forms, their sense of responsibility for the world of culture, their relationships, varying between docile submission and proud independence, with the world of civil authority; or the venerable Orthodox Churches, with their other-worldly mysticism, their spirit of liturgical worship, their submission, by no means incompatible with inner detachment, to the civil power whatever form that power may take. It is hard to perceive a connection between this complex and very human reality and that high and mystical idea of the Church which is presented to us by the New Testament and by Christian thought in all its phases.'[1]

It is hard. And it is also hazardous, if we are in fact talking to men for whom the Church, in any of its aspects, appears today to be irrelevant. 'Definitions of the Church,' says Paul Ferris in his controversial work about the Church of England, 'are usually meant for those who are in it. . . .

[1] MIEGGE, *Visible and Invisible*, ch. 10.

The outsider who asks about the Church is told that he can't understand it unless he's inside it; even, sometimes, that it's impertinent of him to try. . . . Like most institutions,' he concludes, 'it stubbornly presents its two aspects—one to those inside, the other to those outside. I am, of course, an outsider.'[1]

Still, it is a fact, in our generation, that the 'image' of the Church *is* certainly being presented to mankind, and in ways which, before the advent of mass communication, were impossible. The outsider is constantly looking at the Church in his newspapers and on his television screen. He is aware, for instance, of the Vatican Council of 1962 in a way more detailed, more realistic, more human than he could possibly have been a hundred years ago. He is aware of Christian opinion—of agreement and disagreement within the Church —because he actually sees the arguers and hears their arguments on 'Sunday Break' or 'About Religion.' It is all part of the programme which is set out for him at the same time each week. He has not to make any intellectual effort, or any physical effort either, to hear what Christian opinions are floating about: indeed, it is perhaps more effort to get up and switch the set off than to sit in front of it for half an hour and wait for the variety show which follows!

It is a strange paradox that, in a secular age like our own, so much literature and drama is in fact concerned with the Christian view of life or with the tensions between that view and the secular. 'The outsider,' to use Paul Ferris's term, finds the novels of Graham Greene at least as relevant to his own situation as those, say, of John Braine. John Osborne's *Luther* is not seen as an historical study of the reformer so much as a comment on the real issues which make this generation 'angry' today.

There is, in this sort of way—the way of the outsider looking in—a far greater interest in the Christian religion

[1] FERRIS, *The Church of England*, pp. 9 and 26.

than there was in the period between the wars. And yet the vehicle in which that religion is held, the vessel in which it is kept, the historic, institutional organization and organism which is the Church, appears, to the outsider, irrelevant or worse. Why? Perhaps it is because the Church, the institutional Chuch in whatever form it appears, seems to effect a narrowing, a restraining, a hardening on the vitality and freedom of man. Perhaps because the visible Church appears to most people to represent 'religion' in the narrowest sense of the term: 'religion' as an activity which is distinct from the normal activities of life and often appears to condemn them. Or perhaps, more profoundly, it is what made F. D. Maurice write over a hundred years ago: 'The one thought which possesses me most at this time (1844) and, I may say, has always possessed me, is that we have been dosing our people with religion when what they want is not this but the Living God.'[1]

Tonight, then, I want to talk about the Church: the institutional, visible organization or organism to which I belong. And inevitably I am confronted with these difficulties, none of which I can hope to avoid. First, I am an 'insider' not an 'outsider.' I am therefore bound to talk of the Church subjectively, in the first person singular, out of my own experience of it over fifty years of life within it. Secondly, I am an Anglican, and my experience (as opposed to my knowledge) of the Christian Church has come to me through Anglican worship, Anglican fellowship, Anglican tradition. It is bound to be limited—even though, as I hope, I have tried not to let such limitations totally cloud my vision of the Church Universal. Thirdly, it so happens that my own experience of Anglican Christianity has been for many years an experience of the most overwhelming kind—for it has been in the Africa of the present moment. So different, in its challenges and opportunities, from anything else, that it is

[1] Quoted, *Soundings*, edited Vidler, p. 243.

bound to colour my whole approach and everything I have to say.

It would be stupid, if not dishonest, to ignore these influences. Instead, I want to take the risk of being personal, and of talking *first* about the Church as I know it from within: of all that the reality of the Church has meant to me in terms of my own reality. Only then shall I attempt to talk of the Church as part of the whole Truth of God, revealed to man in the Gospel. And although I shall talk as an 'insider' and an Anglican, because I must, I shall talk about things which are part of our world, part of our human experience in this world, part of life itself: and of concern to every one of you sitting in front of me now.

I can remember, then, as clearly as if it were yesterday, standing in a suburban church with my father and mother on December 15th, 1925, and watching the bishop lay his hands upon the heads of boys and girls in the Sacrament of Confirmation, and awaiting my turn to move to the sanctuary step and kneel before him. I can remember it, not as I remember other events of childhood—birthdays, illnesses, pantomimes, holidays—but as a quite definite starting-point in my life: as a moment when, for me at least, something 'happened' which was irrevocable. Something *happened*. But it was not, so far as I can recollect, at all emotionally exciting. I certainly did not experience any sense of 'conversion.' I could not, even faintly, have echoed the words of John Wesley: 'I felt my heart strangely warmed. I felt I did trust in Christ, Christ alone for salvation; and an assurance was given me that he had taken away my sins, even mine. . . .' Indeed (because that was the way I had been brought up by my mother) I had received the assurance of the forgiveness of my sins by making my confession to a priest and receiving absolution at his hands—a practice I have continued from that day to this and shall do, I hope, until I die. 'Father, I have sinned. . . .'

All I am trying to say is that my Confirmation was the beginning of what I can only describe as my *real* life. And it came to me through the Church—in a rather ugly building (as I now realize) in a form of service which was not particularly exciting, and at the hands of an old man whom I never knew, and only saw again in the distance once or twice before he died. In other words, the starting point for my experience of the Christian life was fundamentally and inextricably set in the context of that visible organism . . . it began with what I could see and hear and touch and know with my reason as well as with my heart. And I believed, that behind and within all this external form and pattern, working through it, reaching me through it, calling me through it, was Almighty God. I certainly will not weary you with any 'story of my life'— a very uneventful one by any standards—at school and then here at Oxford. But I can only say that, so far as my Christianity went, it still depended utterly, increasingly, upon the life of the Church wherever I was. I do not mean to say that I accepted and used that life as I might have done. Still less that I made any contribution to it myself. Nor that it was a steady progress. . . . But I learned to worship and to pray, I learned to know myself and to be penitent, I learned, horribly slowly, a little more of the demands of Christian love and Christian compassion—all *within* that institutional, organic structure, the Church. I could not have conceived the Christian life then as being possible 'outside' that community. I cannot conceive it now. Christ to me was, and is, present, knowable, real there, 'where two or three are gathered together' in his name: there, beneath the outward forms of bread and wine . . . 'My body . . . my blood . . . Do this . . .': there, in the words of forgiveness or the words of blessing or the words of authority used by his minister. 'Thy sins are forgiven thee. . . .' 'Go in peace. . . .' '*I* say unto you . . .'

But it was at Oxford, I think, that I first dimly became aware of that other Presence of Christ which has been to me so real a presence ever since. And again it came to me through his Church—or at least through some of those—priests or laymen—who so effectively represented his Church in the Oxford of those days. The 1930s. The time, in England, when mass unemployment was the symptom of a social order that had gone rotten. When 'Hunger Marchers,' thousands of them, walked in their pit-clothes from the coal-mines of South Wales and the dockyards of the North, to Westminster, because life *was* hunger and pain and idleness; without dignity, almost without meaning. The time, in Europe, of the rise of the dictators, the Italian invasion of Abyssinia, the prelude to the Spanish Civil War, to the collapse of the balance of power—the real beginning, though we could not bring ourselves to think of it, of World War. And the Oxford Union passed its most notorious resolution 'That this House will in no circumstances fight for its King and Country.'

It was a time, then, when there were plenty of 'causes': plenty of vital social issues to challenge us: plenty of reasons why, as Christians, we should be 'concerned' or 'committed' or 'involved.' We formed a small Fellowship—in the care of a great priest, Miles Sargent—to try to make at least some gesture as Christians to show that we believed the social order to be God's concern, not Caesar's. We attended Summer Schools of Sociology to learn more about such things as the Marx-Leninist gospel, or the ghastly scandal of slum-housing in London, or just, the Kingdom of God over against the world in which we lived.

I can only say that it was here, at Oxford, very dimly, very feebly, and very intermittently, that I first began to realize that you cannot love the invisible God unless you find him in 'the brother whom you have seen': that, in other words, in more theological jargon, the real presence of Christ in his sacraments is impossible without the real presence of Christ in man.

So—before my ordination to the priesthood—I asked if I might be allowed to test my vocation within the Community of the Resurrection at Mirfield—a community of priests and laymen, accepting the life of poverty, chastity and obedience, and committed ever since its foundation to a way of life which would proclaim the relevance of the Gospel to the modern world. Committed, too, to large-scale missionary work in South Africa and Southern Rhodesia. And there, to Africa, in 1943, I was sent.

Oxford and Mirfield—with a brief interval in a parish in Swindon—and in both contexts, what I can only describe (and of course I cannot compel you to believe me!) as God reaching down to me through human agents, through his ministers, through my brethren in Community, through the discipline of the common life and the rule, through the silence—but *always* through the Church of which all these were part.

Then! Africa! I have spoken already—perhaps too much —of the Christian life in its African context and meaning. I have also written a book. All I want to say now, about South Africa, is this. Race and colour prejudice exist almost everywhere. Certainly they exist in this country: certainly they exist in America—and with less excuse, in both cases, than in South Africa. But for the Christian the challenge lies not where so many think it does—in the bare fact of intolerance and injustice and inflicted misery. It lies far deeper. It lies in the nature of man himself. Or so I believe, and so I came to act in South Africa. For the Christian, racial prejudice is an intolerable evil and has to be fought at every level where it shows itself, because man is made in the image of God: because God, on the Christian definition, has clothed himself in human nature: because any offence against the dignity of man is therefore not an offence against man alone, but a blasphemy, a denial of God's truth, a violation— or an attempted violation of his very person. 'Inasmuch as ye have done it unto one of the least of these ye have done it unto me.'

And now—the new Africa. Tanganyika: so typical of all that is most hopeful and encouraging on that great continent. And my own diocese—a very poor one in material terms— so typical, too, of the work of the Christian Church over the past hundred years. It is so easy to imagine the 'missionary church' as a kind of fussy old aunt, caring for those charming little black children, teaching them the right stories and correcting their wrong ideas about God. So horribly easy to think of the 'missionary church' as a sort of refuge from the dark forces which, at least in the past, were threatening and disturbing simple and unlettered folks and making life a fear and a haunting. So easy to think of the 'missionary church' as a rather shabby, faded copy of the administration —with schools, but not very good schools: hospitals, but rather second-rate hospitals: social services, but serving out somewhat tired and tepid goods. Sometimes, as I go round my diocese, I am tempted to think like this myself. When you have no money, you cannot express your love very splendidly, very gorgeously. You have to make do with mud and stick classrooms and makeshift hospital equipment.

But in fact, in Tanganyika, the *Church* has been the greatest revolutionary force in the country: greater, because working at a deeper level, even than the 'winds of change' which have blown away the colonial past and opened the door to a free and self-determined future. For if you preach the dignity of man: if you proclaim the Fatherhood of God: if you give sacraments which express and sustain Communion—fellow-ship between man and man and between man and God—you are 'turning the world upside down': you are the agent of a revolution whose end is not in sight: you have come, as your Master came, 'not to bring peace, but a sword.' The freedom of Tanganyika, as elsewhere, today rests upon and is sustained by this revolution—expressed in terms of education, of medical care, of social services originally provided by the Christian Church *alone:* only gradually accepted as the responsibility of the State: even, like the democratic principle itself, the fruit and the flower of a gospel lived out in obscurity and discomfort and poverty a hundred years ago: a Gospel expressed in an *institution*, an organism, a system of worship and belief and behaviour: but a gospel at whose heart and centre is the word 'freedom'—for it is a gospel of Love, and Love is not Love unless it is free. 'Jesus, looking upon him, loved him . . .' but he let him go!

This is, I know, a very unorthodox way of talking about the meaning of the Church. It has left unsaid whole areas and aspects of its life which ought to find a place in any study of the Christian way. But I warned you that mine would be an account of an 'insider'—of one, that is, for whom the Church, and in my case the Anglican Church, has been the source, the guardian and the guide, to all the truth I am capable of knowing about God and about man.

But it is necessary to end on a rather different note. To try to say something, however sketchily and unworthily, about the Church as it really is, in itself.

In the writings of the Apostles the Church is described by two metaphors—partly alike, partly contrary to each other. It is described, chiefly by St Paul, as the Body of Christ. But it is also described, in the Revelation of St John, as the Bride of Christ. There is a tension between these two metaphors which takes us to the heart of the mystery of the Church itself.

'The Body of Christ'—'the organ' (to quote Miegge again) 'by means of which Christ continues to be present and to make his influence felt in history. This does not mean that the Church is divine and human in the same *sense* as Christ. . . .

That incomparable moment of the meeting of God with man *has* taken place and is all-sufficient. That remains: and nothing can touch or affect its permanence, as something which has happened once and for all and is irrevocable. The Church, however, lives in the reflection of this event. . . .' The Body of Christ . . . 'a real actual presence of the Lord of the Church, within the Church: "Lo, I am with you all the days . . ." the assurance that it is more'—so *much* more—'than an empirical society, that it bears within itself a divine mystery, a divine destiny, and that the gates of Hell cannot prevail against it.' This is the Church. The *Body* of Christ.

But it is also the Bride . . . in some ways the very antithesis of all that has just been said. 'The Bride is in reality the affianced, who *awaits* the bridegroom "until he come." Up till the present time the Bride has received only the pledges and the first fruits of his presence in the Spirit and the sacramental signs. As things *now* stand Christ is not yet *fully* present in his Church: or rather he is both present *and* expected, and that presence which he now accords is only the promise of that fullness of his presence which belongs to the future.'[1]

Is this a desperately hard thing to understand? But then Christ never promised that his truth would be easy. It is at least one way of explaining that which to so many outsiders like Paul Ferris—like some of you—is the scandal of the Church. Its deep divisions, so contrary to the will and purposes of its Founder—so devastating in their effect upon the witness of the Church to the world. 'That they may be one . . . that the world may believe': the two hang together. But not only the divisions—the pride, the aloofness, the compromise, the self-righteousness, the will to power, the cruelty and the anger in face of heresy and opposition—all these are part of 'the waiting'—in Scriptural terms the marriage (of the Lamb) has not yet taken place. The Church

[1] MIEGGE: op. cit., pp. 127-8

lives between two events, between that Christ who has already come, and 'him who is coming and yet to come.' There *is* imperfection, there *is* inadequacy, there *is* humiliation: all that is meant by 'scandal.' But there is a destiny of glory: and it is for this that the Church is, and is waiting.

There is a marvellously simple description of the Christian Church in its earliest moments which tells us all we need to know of its essential nature:

'They continued steadfastly in the Apostles' teaching and the fellowship, in the breaking of bread and the prayers . . . and the multitude of them that believed were of one heart and soul: and not one of them said that aught of the things which he possessed was his own: but they had all things *common*.'

The Church is the Body of Christ and the Bride of Christ. But the Church is also the Community of Christians 'obediently living the life of love in a world which has no understanding of community and no time for love, though it longs for both.'

This is the Christian vocation; yours and mine. We are called to continue 'steadfastly' against the shifting, changing tides of human affairs.

And to enable us to do this we have 'the breaking of the bread' and 'the prayers.' We have, in fact, what we always most deeply need: community expressed in a *common* act of worship or liturgy, and that act itself catching us up into eternity but also making us 'members one of another.' It is by our faithfulness to this that we shall learn how to be 'steadfast.' It is by our 'steadfastness in the apostles' teaching and fellowship, in the breaking of the bread and in the prayers' that we shall be the Church wherever we are.

VIII. THE HARD CORE

In the course of these addresses, I have more than once quoted from Rose Macaulay's *The Towers of Trebizond*. I make no excuse for doing so again as a kind of preface to what I want to say in conclusion. It is a sentence or two right at the end of her book, and Aunt Dot is talking to her niece, whose lover has been killed in a car smash. . . . 'I know you read Clement of Alexandria: do you remember where he says, "We may not be taken up and transported to our journey's end, but must travel thither on foot, traversing the whole distance of the narrow way?" One mustn't lose sight of the *hard core* which is, do this, do that . . . understand the world you live in and be on terms with it, don't dramatize and dream of *escape*.'

The hard core of Christianity is what we have been trying to think about throughout this week: that, set in the context of the world we live in. I recognize only too clearly that my own attempts to describe this hard core and to make it relevant have been very unworthy and feeble. I warned you, in my first address, that I am no theologian. And moreover, I am horribly aware of the difficulty in our world of 'communication' between Christians and non-Christians, even between one generation and another. 'Understand the world you live in' was easier for those of Aunt Dot's generation than it is for us. For, whatever else may be said, it *is* a more complicated world just because we know so much more about it: just because our knowledge of it is so immediate and without time for reflection. And, because it is complicated, it is perhaps easier to take a gloomy view of it than it used to be. Not only because we have lost our belief in an automatic progress to better and better goals and fulfilments, but because of the real and constant problems which haunt us and cast deep shadows.

Many of these we have touched on this week. They are so obvious, so present to us, that I hardly need to mention them again. The *fear* consequent upon a divided world—divided by differing ideologies, divided between rich and poor, divided by emergent nationalisms. The fear of the *power* that man has himself discovered and can unleash at will. The fear of *vastness* all about us, and our own littleness. The loneliness that all these fears can bring into the human heart.

But fundamentally, because theologically—because, if we may dare to express it so, from God's point of view—the world 'is very good.' And man, because he is man, God's creature, made in God's image and likeness, is also 'very good.' And the things he uses and the things he knows and discovers and invents, because they also are God's creatures, are 'very good.'

This is not fantasy or escapism, nor is it a denial of the realities of Evil and of Sin and of Death. It is simply the assertion of truth about Creation and man as part of Creation. It says nothing of the use that he can make of it if, in his freedom, he so chooses. It sets the mystery of Evil—however we may care to meet that mystery—in the context of a world that is still, and will be till the end of time, God's world. And it can make a difference to the way in which we approach that world and live in it.

In the first place, if we believe that it *is* God's world, we must rejoice in it and expect it to be capable of *enriching* life. Here is the first great paradox of Christianity. We are pledged by our baptismal promises 'to renounce the world, the flesh and the devil.' But this world that we renounce is, precisely, society organized apart from God: is what we understand by the adjective 'worldly' in the pejorative sense. The very renunciation of this world leaves us the more free to rejoice in and to love God's creation—the world which, in everything, bears the traces of his hands and is a continuous reminder of his uncreated loveliness. St Francis of Assisi— the saint most familiar even to our generation—expresses this truth and the paradox that lies behind it. Renunciation: he casts away the wealth and the prestige that are his own worldly heritage, together with the clothes of silk and satin that he throws at his father's feet. He loves his Lady Poverty and follows her to the ends of the earth. He 'bears in his body the marks of the Lord Jesus.' But he is the most world-affirming saint in history: rejoicing in every creature: personalizing every creature (even Death) because he finds in them the person of their Creator.

Perhaps the subtlest temptation of this age—at least here in Europe—is the temptation to despair. If we really 'understand the world we live in' and know it to be still God's world, then we are of all men the most hopeful. 'Marvellous are thy works: and that my soul knoweth right well.'

Therefore, too, we may not only rejoice in this world's goods, but expect to find a purpose and a meaning in it: a purpose and a meaning not *in spite of* the complexity of things—as though we had to push our way through life, like pushing our way through uncleared jungle—but because of the richness and variety of them. We are not created to be men always 'waiting for Godot'—seeing nothing but the passage of time and the meaninglessness of existence. 'For all that may be known of God by men lies plain before their eyes,' wrote the Apostle Paul to the little group of Christian converts in the centre of the world, 'indeed God himself has disclosed it to them. His invisible attributes, that is to say his everlasting power and deity, have been visible ever since the world began . . . in the things he has made. . . . Knowing God, they have refused to honour him as God or to render him thanks. *Hence* all their thinking has ended in futility.'

If all is held in God's hands, is part of Divine wisdom and purpose, then not only can life never be futile, never be meaningless, but it must be invested with a purpose and a meaning so tremendous that it often overwhelms us. Only after the event, only at the top of the ridge, can we pause and look back and understand.

But we must not ask of the world what it cannot give. We must not ask this even of a world which is 'very good' and which is God's creation, sustained by his 'everlasting power and deity.' The men of an earlier generation had a far greater sense of the transience of things than we have. To them the thought of man as a stranger and a pilgrim here on earth, with 'no abiding city,' was as familiar as the thought of death as the gateway to life and joy and peace. It is because of this possessiveness in our attitude to life that we often create our own unhappiness and our own deepest pains and sorrows. We must not ask of the world permanence, changelessness, constancy—for these are not the attributes of the creature but of the Creator with whom alone 'is no variableness, neither shadow of turning.' And if we expect these things and plan and build our life as if they were present, part of the world's fabric and being, then we are certain to lose our way. Every year, on Ash Wednesday, in some village or other of my diocese I go to celebrate the Eucharist. And as the people kneel on the mud floor in front of me, in a church built of earth and wood and thatch, I use the ancient words of the Liturgy and make the sign of the Cross on their foreheads with the ashes: 'Remember O Man, that dust thou art, and unto dust shalt thou return. . . .' Morbid? Medieval? Misanthropic? *No*—just the plain and simple truth. We are here, together, my people and I. But we are only strangers and pilgrims, with no continuing city. The building around us—it will one day return to the dust from which it was made. The floor on which we kneel—perhaps thousands of knees will make their imprint on the dust, but the day will come when it too will return and be unrecognized. And the bodies who kneel in front of me, old men and young women and the babies on their backs peering up at me as I pass . . . 'Dust thou art, and unto dust shalt thou return.' But he whom they kneel to worship, for whom they were created, he will remain the object of that worship for ever. 'Whom have I in heaven but thee, and there is none upon earth'— none, and nothing that I desire in comparison of thee.

Three years ago I had the great privilege of taking part in the Mission to this University conducted by Archbishop Michael Ramsey, the present Archbishop of Canterbury. But I was unable to stay for his final address. As I was considering what I would say to you tonight, and what could be the theme of this evening's talk—what picture I could leave with you from the Gospels—my mind turned to my own favourite chapter in the whole Bible, the thirteenth chapter of St John. And I decided I must use that glorious theme, and no other, as the expression of the True and Living God. But when I turned to the final address in Archbishop Ramsey's book to see what he had chosen, I found he had made precisely the same choice.

My function this week has been chiefly to provide 'a hard core' for you to build on. But I realize that I have not done this so much in terms of actual, hard practicalities, as in ideas. Now I want you to consider the words of Christ as the 'hard core' of your own personal, individual vocation.

I have chosen these verses because they seem to me to contain *all* that we need to know for this purpose.

(a) 'Jesus knowing that his hour was come that he should depart out of this world unto the Father, having loved his own which was in the world, he loved them unto the end' (*EIS TELOS*).

'Jesus, knowing that the Father had given all things into his hands and that he came forth from God and goeth unto God . . .'

Jesus, in other words, *knowing* with a perfection and a completeness that were absolute: *loving* with a love that is perfect and all-embracing—in the light of this knowledge and of this love 'riseth from supper, and layeth aside his garments: and took a towel and girded himself . . . and began to wash the disciples' feet.'

It is significant that this incident of the feet-washing—described with such care and such an eye for detail that it cannot but be the description of an eye-witness—takes the place, in St John, of the action by which the Lord instituted his Eucharist. It is, in fact, a way of interpreting that Eucharist and of laying bare its inner meaning not only to the disciples but—if they are faithful—to the world.

Jesus 'laid aside his garments'—his garments of glory and of godhead—and 'girded himself' with swaddling clothes in the manger: with a purple robe and a crown of thorns before Herod: with the nakedness and stripping of Golgotha—and 'washed their feet'—the feet that are hot and sweaty and dusty with the dirt of the world's streets upon them.

(b) And Simon Peter said, 'Thou shalt never wash my feet.' 'If I wash thee not thou hast no part with me.'

This is the first condition of Christian discipleship—the recognition that we are in need of cleansing: the recognition that always, and in every way we go, we go as sinners, as penitents, and not as the righteous who need no repentance.

What in fact is the quality most needed in a world like ours? A world where man is so haunted and so lonely and so afraid? It is not enough to bring to the service of such a world the qualities of generosity or of understanding alone—desperately as these are needed. For man's condition today needs above all else '*compassion*,' 'suffering with'—'when he came where he was,' there, half-dead and bleeding in the ditch. But you cannot have compassion without penitence. 'If I wash thee not, thou hast no part with me.' Now penitence is not an emotional reaction—nor is it a desperately complicated spiritual exercise. It is something which lies within the reach of every one of us who is capable of loving. It is love. It is an act of the will by which love turns to God again, and, having turned, accepts. 'Lord not my feet only . . .'

(c) 'So when he had washed their feet he said unto them, Know ye what I have done to you? Ye call me Master and Lord: and ye say well—for so I am.'

He is *the Lord:* the Lord of all life, the Master of each one who in penitence acknowledges him. And therefore the first duty of the Christian is *worship*, and the most important work of the Christian is *prayer*. Worship—the acknowledgment of that Lordship, that Sovereignty: and, because we are members one of another, the expression of it corporately as a *worshipping community*.

Even in a divided and fragmented Christendom, even in spite of the scandal of disunity which is still our greatest scandal and greatest stumbling-block in confronting the world, we have preserved corporateness in our own different traditions. Our first duty, surely, is to make *this* corporateness more real, more informed with charity, more of a witness to the love of God which we have known and experienced. And the way to this is faithfulness in common worship. There is no such thing as private prayer. All through this week you have had the opportunity of learning more about the reality of prayer—that is why in these addresses I have said so little about it. 'Ye call me Master and Lord.' . . . Prayer is the supreme way of Christian Action—not a sort of escapist substitute for doing nothing. The Christian faith itself implies 'that the kingdom of God is to be promoted in human history by no other power than the power of love' and 'the power of God's love takes effect in human history in no other way than through the wills and actions of men in whom that love has come to dwell. To pray is to open the heart to the entry of love.'

Of course, it is not easy to pray. Most people who give up prayer do so not because it is perplexing or dark in meaning, but because it is so hard. It is work. It is action. It is demanding: 'It is not easy,' writes John Burnaby, 'to believe that prayer is either always or never answered in the way desired. It is possible—indeed necessary—to believe that true Christian prayer is always the service of God.'[1] 'Ye call me Master and Lord: and ye say well, for so *I am*.'

(d) 'If I then, the Lord and the Master, have washed your feet, ye also ought to wash one another's feet. . . . A servant is not greater than his lord; neither one that is sent greater than he that sent him. . . .'

Service. It is a word too easily used by Christians if they forget what it really means. 'He took a towel'—it was the outward badge of slavery, of humiliation. 'He girded himself'—made the humiliation a reality, by laying aside the garments of his glory and clothing himself with the garments of mortal flesh. 'He washed their feet'—the action, the activity, of the slave: disregarded by those for whom it was done, unrewarded by thanks or recognition of any kind: at worst, disgusting: at best, a drudgery.

So the action of Christians which must flow from their

[1] J. BURNABY, *Soundings*, 232-3.

penitence and their worship is *service*. And it is 'enough for
the disciple that he be as his master, and the servant as his
lord.'

I have come to you from Africa. From one of the countries
in Africa just at the beginning of its history as a sovereign
independent state. But I have also had experience of other
parts of the great continent, richer and more powerful, yet
infinitely less hopeful and less happy. Africa needs, with a
very great urgency, the *service* of the Christian Church. Today,
more even than a hundred years ago, is the day of opportunity.
For now we have the chance of contributing to the full and
free development of new nations: nations of immense
vitality and hopefulness: nations which recognize the divided
world in which they are compelled to live, but which, in the
case of the vast majority, desire above all to contribute to
the healing of division. But countries like Tanganyika,
potentially so rich in human skills and abilities, have been
left desperately poor at the beginning of their day of freedom
in trained manpower. This is, perhaps, the most devastating
criticism of colonialism—that it did not care sufficiently, or
did not act in time, to give back to Africa in exchange for
so much material benefit and power the skills it could so
easily have taught. I speak of Africa, for it is the place I
know and the place I love. But I speak for all countries in
need of development: for all lands confronted—as Tanganyika
is—with the three enemies—poverty, ignorance and disease.
What a field for Christian service! But only if it really *is*
service, and not a disguised form of the thing which seeks
privilege or power or even, only, thanks.

It must be as servants of Africa that we come: recognizing
that we have no claim at all to any other position. The towel
must be our badge, and it must be girded close around us.
And the skills we bring—as doctors or as teachers or as
technicians—these are the instruments of our service: the
basin and the water, if you like, which we must use for the

task. It is to no purpose coming to Africa to serve if you have not the tools of your service—and it may mean years of preparation, perhaps, before you acquire them.

But neither the service, nor the skills—the towel nor the water—will avail anything without faith: to transpose a context a little—'the substance of things *hoped for*, the evidence of things *not seen*.' To be able to go and to give and to use: and at the end of it all, whether after a few years or a lifetime, to be dispensable: this is the faith you require. 'The servant is not greater than his lord, nor he that is sent than he that sent him.' To the worker, the end of that life of service, the moment of completion and consummation appeared to be, and indeed truly was, a single cry in the darkness, from a gallows.

But I hope I am not so foolish as to limit Christian service to one form of activity or to one part of God's world. I am aware, for one thing, of the pace of change: of the fact that in ten years' time, or even in five, our world may be a totally different world and the claims upon Christian compassion and Christian faith will be different too. I am also aware that, even now, I am addressing persons with widely differing aptitudes, characters and talents. It would be an intolerable insult to assume a sort of mass-opinion which could be swayed in one direction or another by some appeal to its generosity. I am aware, above all, that what is right for one may be wrong for another: and that vocation—the Christian vocation at least—must be understood against a background of diversity: of persons, each with his own particular and special place to fill in God's world and in God's purposes.

Service overseas—but also here—in the persons of those who are at once the product of our social order and the 'outsiders'—the maladjusted children, the alcoholics, the neurotics, the delinquents and criminals, the lonely and aged . . .

Vocation! Is there really any way of saying to an audience what it means to each one within that audience?

Vocation! It is—somehow—like 'service' or 'commitment,' a rather dangerous word. It is so easy to talk, and even to think, of '*my* vocation'—as though it was something upon which I confer a dignity and a glory by accepting it.

But what is it really? Once again—remember Early Church: Dawn. Laodicea is one of them—the least attractive, not unlike some of our Christian churches today. 'I know thy works, that thou art neither cold nor hot . . . so because thou art lukewarm, and neither hot nor cold, I will spue thee out of my mouth.' Not a very encouraging thing to hear. And it gets even worse. 'Thou sayest, I am rich (and have gotten riches) and have need of nothing; and knowest not that thou art wretched and miserable and poor and blind and naked.'

Yet it is to *this* church: to this group of Christians— lukewarm in their faith, wretched, miserable, poor, blind and naked in their life as Christians, that the most winning words in the whole of Scripture are addressed:

'Behold, I stand at the door and knock: if any man hear my voice and open the door, I will come in to him and will sup with him, and he with me.'

Vocation! What is it—really? *My* life? *My* activity? *My* decision? *My* way?

It is none of these. It is Jesus, the Lord, the True and Living God, standing, knocking, waiting. That is all.

SCIENCE AND CHRISTIAN BELIEF
C. A. COULSON

Professor Coulson shows that science is a religious activity playing its part in the unfolding of God's purpose.

THE EPISTLE OF PAUL TO THE ROMANS
C. H. DODD

This great Epistle lives for the layman as well as the theologian in a way that no other commentary does.

A SHORT BIBLE, Authorised Version
ARRANGED BY AUSTIN FARRER

'I don't know that I ever learned so much, from anything of the same sort and on the same scale.'   C. S. LEWIS

THE MEANING OF PRAYER
H. E. FOSDICK

This book has shown millions how to pray.

THE SECRET SAYINGS OF JESUS
R. M. GRANT *with* D. N. FREEDMAN

'Excellent. It should be bought and read by all who are interested in the development of early Christianity.'   GUARDIAN

NAUGHT FOR YOUR COMFORT
TREVOR HUDDLESTON

'A noble book, a superb book, to be read by anyone who cares about race or human relations.'   GUARDIAN

THE PERENNIAL PHILOSOPHY
ALDOUS HUXLEY

'It opens doors into aspects of life and thought which most people would never have discovered.'   NATIONAL REVIEW

THE PLAIN MAN'S BOOK OF PRAYERS
WILLIAM BARCLAY

Written specially for Fontana by a distinguished scholar and gifted preacher to help those who wish to pray.

MORE PRAYERS FOR THE PLAIN MAN
WILLIAM BARCLAY

An essential companion to *The Plain Man's Book of Prayers* containing slightly longer daily prayers and Bible readings.

THE PLAIN MAN LOOKS AT THE BEATITUDES
WILLIAM BARCLAY

In working out the implications of the startling paradoxes of the Beatitudes, the author helps to discover the technique of being a Christian.

THE MAN NEXT TO ME
ANTHONY BARKER

'An altogether exceptional exposition of modern missionary endeavour.'
TREVOR HUDDLESTON

LETTERS AND PAPERS FROM PRISON
DIETRICH BONHOEFFER

These documents, smuggled out of prison under the nose of the Gestapo, have a clear and shining unity.

JESUS AND THE WORD
RUDOLPH BULTMANN

An interpretation of the teaching of Jesus by one of the greatest New Testament scholars of our time.

CHRISTIANITY AND HISTORY
HERBERT BUTTERFIELD

'As crystal clear as it is wise and compelling. Sentences cry out to be quoted.'
SPECTATOR